J.K. LASSER'S

HOW YOU CAN PROFIT FROM THE NEW TAX LAWS

NEW EDITION

The J.K. Lasser Tax Institute

Bernard Greisman, Editor

A J.K. Lasser Tax Institute Book

Published by Prentice Hall Press
New York, New York 10023

A J.K. Lasser Tax Institute Book
Published by Prentice Hall Press
A Division of Simon & Schuster, Inc.
Gulf + Western Building
One Gulf + Western Plaza
New York, New York 10023

PRENTICE HALL PRESS is a trademark of Simon & Schuster, Inc.

Manufactured in the United States of America

10 9 8 7 6 5 4 3 2 1

ISBN: 0-13-444050-1

CONTENTS

TRAVEL, ENTERTAINMENT, AND OTHER JOB EXPENSES 87

IRA AND OTHER RETIREMENT PLANS 103

BUSINESS TAXES   127

REVISED DEPRECIATION RULES   149

FARM, TIMBER, ENERGY, AND NATURAL RESOURCES   167

REPORTING REQUIREMENTS AND TAX PRACTICE   177

PROJECTING THE TAX CONSEQUENCES OF THE NEW LAW   187

PREFACE

The first edition of this book was originally written to explain the Economic Recovery Tax Act of 1981, which heralded the largest three-year tax cut in history. However, within 12 months, Congress moved with unprecedented speed to enact the Tax Equity and Fiscal Responsibility Act of 1982, which scheduled one of the largest tax increases in history and included a major revision of the tax rules for company retirement plans. A few months later, another act corrected and amended laws passed during the year. In 1983, new legislation subjected Social Security benefits to tax for the first time. When Congress passed the 1984 Tax Act, it was the most complex tax measure passed in 30 years. The Act took back some of the benefits provided by the earlier tax acts, added some new ones, and generally managed to make an already complicated law much more complex. Before this legislation could be digested, however, the administration in 1985 asked for a wholesale revision of the tax laws. After a year of debate, Congress passed the 1986 Tax Act, which further complicates tax reporting for many taxpayers and generally favors the Treasury. There are promised tax reductions, but these may not materialize if Congress reconsiders its policy during 1987 and 1988. In any event, every taxpayer is affected by the act, and you should be aware of how it affects your personal, investment, and business decisions. We have prepared this book to help you in this task.

We are grateful to Elliott Eiss, member of the New York Bar, who shared in the preparation of this book.

Bernard Greisman
Editor, J. K. Lasser Tax Institute

HIGHLIGHTS OF THE 1986 TAX ACT

Tax Item	Prior Law	New Law
Tax Rates	Fifteen tax brackets above the zero bracket amount (ZBA) ranging from 11 to 50 percent.	Two tax brackets with rates of 15 and 28 percent becoming effective in 1988, with a five percent surcharge to eliminate 15 percent benefit for middle and high income taxpayers. In 1987, a five-bracket rate schedule ranging from 11 to 38.5 percent.
Passive loss restrictions	Losses from tax shelter investments and businesses in which an investor did not materially participate were deductible from all sources of income.	Losses from passive activities are deductible only from income of similar passive activities. They are not deductible from salary or investment income such as interest and dividends unless the activity comes within certain exceptions such as a working interest in oil and gas property. Losses that would be disallowed as passive losses are partially deductible under a phaseout schedule of 65 percent in 1987, 40 percent in 1988, 20 percent in 1989, and 10 percent in 1990. To qualify for the phaseout, the activity generally must have been entered into on or before October 22, 1986. Rental activities are considered passive. However, a special $25,000 loss allowance is allowed for rental losses if your AGI is under $100,000 and you perform some managerial work. The loss allowance is phased out between an AGI of $100,000 and $150,000.

Tax Item	Prior Law	New Law
Zero bracket amount (standard deduction)	The following zero bracket amounts applied in 1986: Filing status: <u> ZBA</u> Joint returns $3,670 Head of household 2,480 Single individuals 2,480 The ZBA was integrated in the tax schedules.	Standard deduction is not integrated in tax schedules but deducted from adjusted gross income if itemized deductions are not claimed. <u>1987</u> <u>1988</u> Married $3,760 $5,000 Single 2,540 3,000 Household 2,540 4,400 Extra deductions are allowed for elderly and blind who may in 1987 claim amounts scheduled for 1988.
Personal Exemption	The exemption was $1,080. Extra exemption for age and blindness.	In 1987, $1,900; in 1988, $1,950; in 1989, $2,000. No extra exemptions for age or blindness. Person claimed as exemption by others may not claim personal exemption. Benefits of personal exemption to be lost in high tax bracket in 1988.
Married, two-earner deductions	Ten percent of lower earnings up to $3,000.	Not allowed.
Income averaging	Low marginal rates to part of income that was 140 percent higher than prior three years average.	Not allowed.

Foreign income exclusion	Up to $80,000 of earned income may be tax free.	Starting after 1986, exclusion reduced to $70,000 and may not be allowed to U.S. citizens and residents working in areas with State Department travel restrictions such as Libya, Cuba, Vietnam, and North Korea.
U.S. Government employees in Panama	Court cases held that U.S. employees of Panama Canal Commission were exempt from U.S. tax under a treaty.	U.S. employees of the Panama Canal Commission are not exempt from U.S. taxes, but may receive tax-free allowances similar to those available for employees of the State Department stationed in Panama.
Foster care payments	A foster parent who receives reimbursements from a governmental agency for the cost of caring for a foster child in the home of the foster parent may exclude payments if the expenses were accounted for.	The exclusion applies also to payments reserved for the cost of caring for a foster adult. A parent need not meet the accounting requirement to claim the exclusion. These rules apply starting with returns for 1986 to be filed in 1987.
Investment income of a minor child	If income-producing assets were transferred to a minor child, income earned on those assets generally was taxed to the child at the child's marginal rate.	All of the unearned income of a child under age 14 that is over $1,000 is taxed to the child at the top marginal rate of his or her parents. The rule applies to income earned on property transferred by a parent or other person.
Personal exemptions and zero bracket amount	Both the child and the parents may claim a personal exemption on their respective tax returns. The zero bracket amount generally was not allowed	The personal exemption is not allowed to an individual who may be claimed as a dependent on another taxpayer's return—for example, where a

Tax Item	Prior Law	New Law
	to a child who had investment income and was claimed as an exemption.	child is eligible to be claimed as a dependent by a parent. A child may claim a limited standard deduction amount.
Individual estimated tax payments	Individuals owing tax who do not have sufficient taxes withheld from their wages must make estimated tax payments. These payments must equal at least the lesser of 100 percent of last year's tax liability, or 80 percent of the current year's liability.	Increases percentage of current year's tax liability to 90 percent.
Individual capital gains	An individual may deduct from gross income 60 percent of net capital gain (the excess of net long-term capital gain over any net short-term capital loss). In 1986, when the maximum regular individual tax rate was 50 percent, the deduction provided a maximum net capital gain tax of 20 percent.	No capital gain deduction after 1986. Long-term capital gain is subject to ordinary income tax rates. However, the law retains the distinction between long- and short-term capital gains for purposes of placing a 28 percent tax ceiling on long-term capital gain. Capital loss treatment remains the same. Capital losses deductible from other income is limited up to $3,000 a year. Excess losses are carried over.
Grantor trusts	Under certain circumstances, the grantor is taxed directly on trust income when treated as owner of the trust, i.e., if the grantor:	The 10-year exception for grantor trusts is repealed. A grantor trust exists when the grantor has a reversionary interest (at the time of transfer) of

(1) Has a reversionary interest expected to return to him or her within 10 years;
(2) Has the power to control beneficial enjoyment of the income or corpus;
(3) Retains certain administrative powers;
(4) Retains the right to revoke the trust at any time during the first 10 years of the trust's existence; or
(5) The income of the trust may be distributed to the grantor or grantor's spouse during the first 10 years of the trust's term.

more than five percent of the value of the property transferred to the trust. Further, a grantor is treated as holding a reversionary interest held by a spouse if the spouse is living with the grantor. The new rules apply to trust transfers made after March 1, 1986. An exception applies to the 10-year trusts created pursuant to a binding property settlement entered into before March 2, 1986, which required the taxpayer to establish a grantor trust.

Scholarship and fellowships

Degree candidates at an educational institution may exclude amounts received as a scholarship or fellowship grant, and also incidental amounts for expenses for travel, research, clerical help, and equipment.

Non-degree candidates may exclude only scholarship or fellowship grants from tax-exempt organizations or international or governmental agencies limited to a maximum lifetime exclusion of $10,800.

Payments for teaching or other services required as a condition of receiving the grant to degree candidates is tax free if all candidates for a particular degree must perform such services.

Exclusion limited to degree candidates and amounts paid for tuition and course-related fees, books, and supplies. All other payments are taxable. New rule applies to grants made after August 16, 1986, in taxable years starting after 1986.

Tax Item	Prior Law	New Law
Consumer interest	Allowed as an itemized deduction.	Phased out over a five-year period. The deductible is 65 percent in 1987; 40 percent in 1988; 20 percent in 1989; and 10 percent in 1990. No deduction after 1990.
Mortgage interest	Allowed as an itemized deduction.	Deduction limited to mortgages on first and second residences. Restrictions on use of proceeds for medical and education where loan exceeds cost of residence plus improvements. Rule applies after 1986 to mortgage loans made after August 16, 1986.
Charitable deduction for non-itemizers	For 1986, non-itemizers may deduct charitable contributions.	Repealed after 1986.
Itemized deductions for state and local taxes	Itemized deductions are allowed for the following state and local taxes: income taxes, real property taxes, personal property taxes, and sales taxes.	Repealed after 1986. Adoption Assistance Program in Title 12 of Social Security Act will provide matching funds for adoption administrative fees.
Adoption expenses	Deduction of up to $1,500 of adoption fees and expenses for adoption of a child with special needs.	Repealed after 1986. Adoption Assistance Program in Title 12 of Social Security Act will provide matching funds for adoption administration fees.

Mortgage interest and taxes allocable to tax-free allowance for ministers and military personnel	An IRS ruling held that a minister may not deduct mortgage interest and property taxes allocable to a tax-free parsonage allowance.	Ministers receiving tax-free parsonage allowances, as well as military personnel receiving tax-free military housing allowances, may deduct mortgage interest or real property taxes on the taxpayer's residence. Rule is retroactive to 1986.
Investment interest	Investment interest equal to the total of the following items was deductible: 1. $10,000 allowance. 2. Net investment income. In addition to the $10,000 allowance, you may deduct interest that does not exceed net investment income. Any disallowed interest is carried over to the next year and treated as investment interest paid or accrued in that year and is again subject to the above limitation.	Investment interest is deductible only to the extent of net investment income after 1990. Before then, the first $10,000 of investment interest exceeding investment income is partially deductible at 65 percent in 1987; 40 percent in 1988; 20 percent in 1989; and 10 percent in 1990. Disallowed interest may be carried forward if there is investment income in excess of net investment interest in the later year. In calculating net investment income, interest expenses and income attributable to tax shelters and other passive activities subject to the loss limitation rules are disregarded. However, if a loss is allowed under the five-year phaseout rule for passive losses, the loss will reduce investment income for purposes of figuring the investment interest deduction.
Medical expenses	Deductible if more than five percent of adjusted gross income.	Deductible if more than 7.5 percent of adjusted gross income. Special deduction for home and car improvements made to facilitate the movement of handicapped persons.

Tax Item	Prior Law	New Law
Meal expenses	"Quiet business meal" rule under which meal expenses are deductible if meal takes place in settings conducive to business discussion.	Starting in 1987, only 80 percent of allowable business meal expenses are deductible. Further, no deduction is allowed unless business discussion related to a specific business transaction or arrangement takes place.
Entertainment expenses	Deductible if directly related to conducting business or directly preceding or following business discussion.	Eighty percent of allowable business entertainment expenses is deductible. Ticket costs above face value are not deductible except in the case of certain charitable fund-raising events.
Educational travel	Deductible if travelling itself qualifies as a form of education and maintains or improves employment skills or is required by an employer.	Not deductible if travel is only a form of education.
Travel expenses for conventions	The cost of attending a convention or seminar, either for business or for investment purposes, is generally deductible.	Not allowed for travel to nonbusiness conventions such as investment seminars.
Luxury cruises	Business travel expenses while away from home are deductible. No special limit on business trip taken on a cruise ship.	Deductible cost of cruise may not exceed double the highest federal per diem amount allowed to government employees traveling away from home. This rule does not change the rule for attending conventions held on cruise ships, provided the cruise ship is registered in the U.S. and stops at ports of call only in the U.S.

Miscellaneous itemized deductions	Union dues, work clothes, tax preparation fees, and investment expenses are deductible as miscellaneous deductions.	Miscellaneous deductions for union dues, professional journals, and investment expenses, as well as deductions for unreimbursed employee business expenses, are allowable only to the extent they exceed two percent of adjusted gross income.
Unreimbursed travel expenses	Unreimbursed travel expenses are deductible in adjustment section of Form 1040 as above-the-line deductions.	Unreimbursed travel expenses are treated as miscellaneous deductions subject to the two percent AGI limit.
Moving expenses	Deductible in adjustment schedule of Form 1040 as above-the-line deduction.	Deductible as an itemized deduction, but is not subject to two percent of AGI floor. Individual who claims standard deduction may not deduct the moving expenses.
Home office expenses	An employee may claim an itemized deduction for use of a home office as long as the office is used regularly and exclusively for business. The deduction may not exceed the taxpayer's gross income from the business. A court held that these rules do not apply when an employee leases a portion of his home to his employer.	Home office deductions may not exceed net income from the activity; deductions not allowed because of income limit may be carried forward. No deductions are allowed to employees who lease part of their home to an employer.
Hobby losses	Hobby losses are restricted to the amount of hobby income. An activity is presumed not to be a hobby if it is profitable in two out of five consecutive years, or two out of seven years for horse breeding or racing.	An activity (other than horse breeding or racing) is presumed not to be a hobby if it is profitable in three out of five consecutive years; prior law rule is retained for horse activities.

Tax Item	Prior Law	New Law
Political contributions tax credit	Maximum allowable credit is $50 for an individual and $100 for a married couple filing a joint return.	Not allowed.
Unemployment insurance benefits	Limited exclusion.	No exclusion.
Alternative minimum tax	The alternative minimum tax (AMT) is designed to recoup tax benefits that have reduced or eliminated your regular income tax. AMT is imposed if it exceeds your regular income tax or you have no tax liability after claiming certain tax deductions or credits.	Retained
Rate	20 percent.	21 percent.
Exemption amount	$40,000 for joint returns, $30,000 for singles.	The $40,000 exemption for joint returns and $30,000 for single filers is reduced 25 cents for each $1 that the minimum joint taxable income exceeds $150,000 ($112,500 for single individuals). The effect of the exemption reduction is to increase AMT to 26 percent. After 1986, the untaxed appreciation on charitable contributions of property and interest paid on tax-exempt bonds for nonessential private functions issued after August 7, 1986, will be an AMT preference item.

Spousal IRA	You are allowed an additional deduction for contributions to an IRA for the benefit of your spouse if (1) the spouse has no compensation for the year, (2) the spouse has not attained aged 70-1/2, and (3) you file a joint income tax return for the year. If these tests are met, the annual deduction limit is increased from $2,000 to $2,250. The contribution may be divided as you choose, provided the contribution for neither spouse exceeds $2,000. If both have compensation, including compensation less than $250, the spousal deduction is not allowed.	The pre-1987 limit of $2,250 for deductible contributions remains. However, the requirement that a spouse have no income for the $250 contribution is repealed for tax years beginning after 1985.
Regular IRAs	Deductible contribution allowed although you are a member of an employer retirement plan.	*No plan coverage.* If you are not an active participant in an employer plan for taxable years after 1986, you may deduct IRA contributions of up to $2,000 as under prior law. If you are married, the prior deduction rules apply if neither spouse is an active participant in an employer plan. The maximum contribution remains $2,000 per working spouse, or $2,250 if there is only one working spouse. *Employer plan coverage.* As an unmarried person covered by an employer plan, you may claim a full IRA deduction after 1986 if your adjusted gross income is below $25,000. If you are married filing jointly where either spouse is covered by an employer plan, you may deduct IRA contributions if joint adjusted gross income is below $40,000.

Tax Item	Prior Law	New Law
		The deduction is phased out for singles with adjusted gross income of more than $25,000, but less than $35,000, and for couples filing jointly with adjusted gross income of more than $40,000, but less than $50,000. No deduction is allowed for taxpayers with adjusted gross incomes exceeding those ceilings unless they are not participants in an employer plan. To the extent deductible IRA contributions are not allowed, a nondeductible contribution may be made. Income earned on an IRA account accumulates tax-free until withdrawn. Starting in 1987, IRA investments may be made in gold or silver coins issued by the U.S. government.
Additional tax on early IRA withdrawals	Amounts withdrawn from an IRA prior to age 59-1/2, death, or disability of the owner are subject to a 10 percent additional income tax.	IRA distributions after 1986 that are made before age 59-1/2, disability, or death, generally will remain subject to a 10 percent penalty. However, withdrawals allocable to nondeductible contributions will not be subject to the penalty. Further, no penalty will be applied for payments before age 59-1/2 that are part of an annuity for life or the joint lives of the taxpayer and a beneficiary.

Item	Present Law	New Law
Qualified cash or deferred arrangements (sec. 401(k)) plans	An employee who has a choice of receiving current pay or having that pay deferred under a profit-sharing or stock bonus plan (or certain pre-ERISA money purchase pension plans) is not taxed as though the compensation has been received. Deferral may be up to $30,000.	The maximum amount that can be deferred under all cash or deferred arrangements in which an employee participates is limited to $7,000. After 1987, the $7,000 cap is adjusted for inflation by reference to percentage increases in the dollar limit under a defined benefit plan.
Lump-sum retirement benefit: 10-year averaging and pre-1974 capital gains treatment	Certain lump-sum distributions received under a qualified plan may qualify for special 10-year averaging and capital gain treatment on the pre-1974 contribution.	Five-year averaging after the age of 59-1/2. However, 10-year averaging is allowed under transitional rules to those aged 50 or over as of January 1, 1986. Pre-1974 capital gain treatment is phased out over a six-year period beginning January 1, 1987.
Incentive stock options	An employee is not taxed on the exercise of an incentive stock option and is entitled to capital gains when the stock is sold. For options to qualify as incentive stock options, the options must be exercisable in the order they are granted, and the employer may not grant the employee such options to acquire stock with a value of more than $100,000 (increased by certain carryover amounts) in any one year.	The requirement that the options be exercisable in the order granted is repealed. The $100,000 limitation is modified to apply to options first exercisable during the year.
First-year expensing	Taxpayers may elect to expense up to $5,000 of the cost of personal business equipment. The $5,000 ceiling was scheduled to increase to $7,500 for taxable years beginning in 1988 and	The ceiling is increased to $10,000 starting in 1987. However, for every dollar of qualifying investment in excess of $200,000, the $10,000 limit is reduced by one dollar.

Tax Item	Prior Law	New Law
	1989, and $10,000 for years beginning after 1989.	
Business credits	An investment credit is allowed for up to 10 percent of investments in tangible personal property.	The regular investment tax credit is repealed for taxable years beginning after December 31, 1985, except for property contracted for at the end of 1985 and put into service by certain dates. Credits on transition property and credit carryovers are subject to a 35 percent reduction for taxable years starting on or after July 1, 1987. For calendar year taxpayers, the 1987 reduction is 17.5 percent.

Starting in 1986, the overall limit for the general business credit is reduced to $25,000 plus 75 percent of the tax liability in excess of $25,000, instead of 85 percent of the excess as under prior law. The limit applies to the sum of the investment credit, if available for 1986, the targeted jobs credit, alcohol fuels credit, and employee stock ownership (ESOP) credit. The ESOP credit is generally repealed for compensation paid after 1986.

Further, the credit for increasing research and development expenses is made subject to the general business credit limit starting in 1986, with the research credit rate reduced from 25 to 20 percent; after 1986, more favorable credit rules will apply to expenditures for basic research. |

The targeted jobs credit is reduced for workers hired after 1985. The 1986 credit is 40 percent instead of 50 percent of the first $6,000 of wages paid in the first year. The 25 percent credit for second-year wages is repealed.

Depreciation

ACRS property generally was grouped in the following classes:

The three-year class: Property with an ADR midpoint of four years or less (such as cars and light-duty trucks), *plus* property used in connection with research and experimentation, and certain horses. Method is 150 percent declining balance, switching to straight line, over three years.

The five-year class: All tangible personal property not included in any other class. Includes railroad track, commercial passenger aircraft, and single-purpose agricultural structures. Method is 150 percent declining balance, switching to straight line, over five years.

The ten-year class: Public utility property with an ADR midpoint of 18.5 to 25 years, certain burners and boilers with an ADR midpoint of 25 years, and mobile homes. Method is 150 percent declining balance, switching to straight line, over 10 years.

The 15-year utility class: Other public utility property with an ADR midpoint of more than 25 years. Method is 150 percent declining balance, switching to straight line, over 15 years.

Under a new accelerated depreciation system, property would be grouped in the following classes:

The three-year class: ADR midpoints of four years and less, excluding automobiles and light trucks, and retaining prior law for horses that are in the three-year class. Method is 200 percent declining balance.

The five-year class: ADR midpoints of more than four years and less than 10 years. Includes autos and light trucks. Method is 200 percent declining balance.

The seven-year class: ADR midpoints of 10 years and less than 16 years. Includes office furniture and fixtures. Method is 200 percent declining balance.

The ten-year class: ADR midpoints of 16 years and less than 20 years. Method is 200 percent declining balance.

The 27.5-year class: Residential real property. Method is straightline.

The 31.5-year class: Non-residential real property (real property that is not residential rental property and that does not have an ADR midpoint of less than 27.5 years). Method is straightline.

Tax Item	Prior Law	New Law
	The 15-year real property class: Low-income housing. Method is 200 percent declining balance, switching to straight line, over 15 years. **The 19-year real property class:** Buildings and structures. ADR lives not assigned to buildings. Method is 175 percent declining balance, switching to straight line, over 19 years.	
Autos annual caps on depreciation	Limitations: $3,200 for the first recovery year, and $4,800 for each succeeding taxable year in the recovery period.	Limitations: $2,560 the first year; $4,100 the second year; $2,450 the third year; and $1,475 in later years.

PERSONAL TAXES

NEW TAX RATES PROMISE
TAX REDUCTIONS

The new law sets two bracket rates of 15 percent and 28 percent which become effective in 1988. In 1987, an interim five-bracket rate structure applies. The lower 15 percent bracket in 1988 may not benefit middle and high income taxpayers. To eliminate the 15 percent tax benefit built into the tax schedule, a five percent surcharge will be imposed on taxable income within a specific range. Further, an additional five percent surcharge also will eliminate the benefit of personal exemptions. On income subject to these surcharges, you will in effect be subject to a rate of 33 percent instead of 28 percent.

Whether or not the new tax rates will give you a tax savings depends on the effect of the new law on the amount of your taxable income. You may wind up with a larger tax if your taxable income is increased by the loss of prior tax benefits. Tax rates schedules and a worksheet for tax liability comparisons are at the end of the book under **Projecting the Tax Consequences of the New Law.**

DEPENDENCY EXEMPTIONS
INCREASED

Each exemption you claim on your return is the equivalent of the following deductions:

In	Deduction for each exemption is:
1987	$1,900
1988	$1,950
1989	$2,000

You claim an exemption for—

Yourself.   Every taxpayer is allowed one exemption. However, starting in 1987, if you are claimed as an exemption by another person, you may not claim a personal exemption for yourself. This rule will prevent your child from claiming an exemption on his or her return if you claim the child as an exemption.

Your spouse.   You claim your spouse as an exemption when you file a joint return. If you file a separate return, you claim your spouse as an exemption if he or she has no income and is not a dependent of another person.

Parents, other relatives and dependents.   As long as you satisfy four tests for each dependent, there is no limit to the number of dependents you may claim.

Test 1.   Relative or member of household.
A qualifying relative may be your:

Child, grandchild, great grandchild, or stepchild;
Brother, sister, half-brother, half-sister, stepbrother or
   stepsister;
Parent, grandparent, great grandparent or stepparent;
Brother or sister of your father or mother;
Son or daughter of your brother or sister;
Father-in-law, mother-in-law, son-in-law, daughter-in-law,
   brother-in-law, or sister-in-law.

A qualifying member of your household may be any person, whether or not related, who made your home his or her principal residence for the entire year and is a member of your household (except if the relationship between you and such person violates state law).

Test 2.   Your support.
You either contribute more than half the dependent's support, or contribute more than 10 percent and, together with others, contribute more than half.

Test 3.   Dependent's gross income.
Your dependent must have less than $1,900 in 1987 ($1,950 in 1988, $2,000 in 1989). This income test does not apply if the dependent is your child who is under 19 or a full-time student, in

which case the amount of his of her gross income may exceed the income floor.

Test 4.   Dependent's citizenship or resident status.

Your dependent must be a United States citizen or national, or a resident of the United States, Canada, or Mexico.

Further, you may not claim an exemption for a dependent who files a joint return unless the joint return is used merely to get a refund of withheld taxes and the income of each spouse is under the income limits required for filing a return.

Starting in 1987, no extra exemptions are allowed for blindness or for being 65 or over.

Exemption phaseout.   In 1988, exemptions will be phased out for single individuals with taxable income of $89,560 or more; for married couples filing jointly, the phaseout begins at taxable income of $149,250. For every $10,920 of taxable income in 1988 above $89,560 or $149,250, one personal exemption is totally phased out. Thus, if a married couple claims four exemptions on a 1988 joint return, the four $1,950 personal exemptions will be completely phased out at a taxable income of $192,930. Beginning in 1989, the income range subject to the phaseout rule will be adjusted for inflation, and the $10,920 phaseout amount per exemption will be increased to $11,200.

NEW STANDARD DEDUCTION

Under pre-1987 law, the equivalent of a standard deduction was incorporated in the tax rates and was called the zero bracket amount. Consequently the amount of the deduction did not have to be calculated, if you did not claim itemized deductions. If you claimed itemized deductions, you had to subtract the ZBA from an itemized deduction and were allowed to deduct the balance of your deduction called excess itemized deductions. The new law replaces the zero bracket amount with the following standard deduction amounts:

In	Married (joint)	Single	Head of Household
1987*	$3,760	$2,540	$2,540
1988	5,000	3,000	4,400

*If you are 65 or over or blind in 1987, take the standard deduction amounts listed for 1988 plus the extra $600 or $750 deduction discussed below.

Married individuals who file separately may claim a $1,880 standard deduction in 1987; $2,500 in 1988. Both spouses must either claim the standard deduction or itemized deductions. If one spouse itemizes on a separate return, the other spouse may not claim any standard deduction.

For each married spouse and surviving spouse who is 65 or older or blind, an extra $600 may be added to the standard deduction. If you are single, an extra $750 may be added for being 65 or older or blind. If both elderly and blind, the extra deduction is $1,200 for married persons and $1,500 for unmarried persons. Thus, in 1987, a single taxpayer over the age of 65 will be allowed a $3,750 deduction ($3,000 plus $750). Starting in 1989, the 1988 deduction amounts and the extra $600 and $750 deduction for the aged or blind will be adjusted for inflation. The extra $600 deduction is not allowed to a married person filing separately where the other spouse itemizes deductions.

You will claim the standard deduction only if your itemized deductions for charitable donations, certain local taxes, interest, allowable casualty loss, miscellaneous expenses, and medical expenses are less than the standard deduction.

EXAMPLE—

You are single and your adjusted gross income is $15,000. Your itemized deductions total $2,000. In 1986, your zero bracket amount is $2,480, thus you do not claim excess itemized deductions. You figure your tax after deducting a personal exemption of $1,080 from your adjusted income.

Adjusted gross income	$15,000
Less exemption	1,080
Taxable income	$13,920

The zero bracket amount is built into tax tables from which you take the tax applied to taxable income of $13,920.

In 1987, you deduct the standard deduction from adjusted gross income.

Adjusted gross income	$15,000
Less standard deduction	2,540
	$12,460
Less exemption	1,900
Taxable income	$10,560

A special standard deduction rule applies to dependents. Under pre-1987 law, a dependent may use the zero bracket to offset earned income but not unearned income. In 1987, a dependent may use up to $500 of the standard deduction to offset unearned income such as interest or dividends. For further details, *see* discussion of income splitting in **Family Income Planning.**

ADJUSTED GROSS INCOME FOR 1987

The term adjusted gross income is used often in this text. It is the amount used in figuring the new two percent floor for the miscellaneous expenses, the new 7.5 percent floor for medical expenses, the 10 percent floor for personal casualty and theft losses, and the charitable contribution limitation. Adjusted gross income is the difference between gross income (Step 1) and deductions (Step 2) listed below. If you do not have any of these deductions, adjusted gross income is the same as gross income.

Step 1. Figure gross income. This is all income received by you from any source, such as wages, salary, gross business income, income from sales and exchanges, interest and dividends, rents, royalties, annuities, pensions, and the like. Gross income does not include such items as tax-free interest from state or local bonds, tax-free parsonage allowance, tax-free insurance proceeds, gifts and inheritances, Social Security benefits which are not subject to tax, tax-free scholarship grants, tax-free board and lodging allowance, and the first $5,000 of death benefits.

Step 2. Deduct from gross income only the following items:

- Trade or business expenses. These are listed on Schedule C.
- Certain travel expenses of employees. Expenses here include reimbursed local transportation expenses, travel expenses away from home and outside salesperson expenses, and certain expenses of performing artists. If you are an employee, do not include unreimbursed travel and entertainment expenses here.
- Net operating losses.
- Certain deductions of life tenants and income beneficiaries of property.
- Contributions to a Keogh plan. The deduction for the contribution on your behalf is taken on Form 1040; contributions for your employees on Schedule C.
- Deductible contributions to IRAs.
- Contributions to pension plans of S corporations.
- Alimony payments.
- Forfeit penalties because of a premature withdrawal of funds from time savings accounts or deposits.
- Expenses to produce rent and royalty income.
- Repayment of supplemental unemployment benefits required because of receipt of readjustment allowances.

- Reforestation expenses.

Step 3. The difference between Steps 1 and 2 is adjusted gross income.

EARNED INCOME CREDIT INCREASE

A special tax credit for low income workers with families may provide a refund or subsidy of $800 in 1987. In 1986, the top credit was $550. An "earned income credit" is available only to low income workers who have dependent children and maintain a household. The credit is designed to encourage low income wage earners to file income tax returns. The credit is a form of negative income tax. Even if no tax withholdings have been taken from your wages and you do not have to file a return because you do not meet the gross income filing requirements, you may receive a payment from the federal government. If you have a tax liability, the credit will be first applied against your tax liability. Any excess credit is refunded to you. Alternatively you may elect to have your credit figured into your withholding to receive advanced payment of the credit throughout the year.

The credit is based only on "earned income," wages, salaries and other employee compensation, plus earnings from self-employment. Starting in 1987, the maximum credit is $800 or 14 percent of your first $5,714 of earned income. If you have income over $5,714, the credit is reduced by 10 percent of the excess over $6,500. Thus, the credit is eliminated when your income reaches $14,500. For 1987, the $5,714 and $6,500 amounts may be increased by an inflation factor. Starting in 1988, the phase out range will be $9,000 to $17,000, although these amounts could be increased by an inflation adjustment.

You do not figure the credit; you find your credit in special tables included in the government's instructions to the tax forms.

The credit will affect benefits under federal assistance programs.

You are eligible for the credit if you are:

(1) Married and entitled to a dependency exemption for a child;

(2) A surviving spouse; or

(3) Head of household (an unmarried child in your household need not be your dependent, but a married child must be your dependent).

Earned income includes all wages, salaries, tips, and other compensation, plus net earnings from self-employment and pro rata share of partnership income. Net self-employment income of less than $400 qualifies as earned income even though not subject to the self-employment tax.

NEW SCHOLARSHIP AND GRANT RULES

The new law distinguishes between grants made before August 17, 1986, and those made after August 16, 1986. Under the new law and starting in 1987, scholarships and fellowships granted after August 16, 1986, are tax free only for degree candidates, and only to the extent the grant pays for tuition and course-related fees, books, supplies, and equipment. Amounts for room, board, and incidental expenses are taxable. Further, no tax-free exclusion is allowed for grants or tuition reductions that pay for teaching or other services. No exclusion is allowed for federal grants where the recipient agrees to future work with the federal government.

Degree Test.   Under the law, scholarships given to students attending a primary or secondary school, or pursuing a degree at a college or university, meet the degree test. Also qualifying is a student (whether full-time or part-time) who receives a scholarship for study at an educational institution that (1) provides an educational program acceptable for full credit towards a higher degree, or offers a program of training to prepare students for gainful employment in a recognized occupation, and (2) is authorized under federal or state law to provide such a program and is accredited by a nationally recognized accreditation agency.

In case of a scholarship or fellowship granted after August 16, 1986, and before January 1, 1987, any amount of such scholarship or fellowship grant received prior to January 1, 1987, and attributable to pre-1987 expenses (such as tuition, room, and pre-1987 costs) may qualify as tax-free benefits.

Rules for pre-August 17, 1986, grants.   After 1986, the following favored tax rules still apply to pre-August 17, 1986, grants.

If you are a degree candidate, the following amounts paid under a grant are tax free: Tuition, matriculation fees, room, board, laundry and other services, and family allowances.

Studies leading to your certification to practice a profession, such as psychiatric nurse, are not equivalent to being a candidate for a degree.

Work-study programs.   Tuition and work payments are tax free if your college requires all its students to take part in the work-study program. Payments for services not required by the program are taxable.

Travel and other expenses.   You are not taxed on allowances specifically designated for expenses incident to the grant, such as for travel (including meals and lodging while traveling and family travel allowance), research, clerical help, and equipment. You are taxable to the extent the allowance is not spent for these purposes.

Payments for teaching or research.   Where the primary purpose of teaching or research is to further your own training and education, payment for such services is tax free if the services are required of all degree candidates. Where the primary purpose is to pay you for services, the payments are taxable, even if teaching or research is required for the degree. Where you are paid for services not required of all degree candidates, a portion of the grant attributable to the services is taxed according to the rate paid for similar services.

If you are not working for a degree, your scholarship or fellowship grant made before August 17, 1986, is tax free up to $300 a month for each month during the year in which you receive payments under the grant. You may claim the $300-a-month exclusion for only 36 months during your lifetime. The months do not have to run consecutively. A grant does not qualify for this tax-free exclusion if it represents payment for services, or for research or studies primarily for the grantor's benefit. After you exclude income for 36 months, all further grants are taxable.

Who makes the grant. To qualify for the 36-month exclusion on a pre-August 17, 1986, grant, the grant must be received from one of the following sources:

(1) The United States, or any agency or instrumentality of the United States.
(2) A state territory, or possession of the United States, or any of their sub-divisions, or the District of Columbia.
(3) A tax-exempt, nonprofit organization operated exclusively for religious, charitable, scientific, literary, testing for public safety, prevention of cruelty to children or animals, or educational purposes.
(4) A foreign government.
(5) An organization under the Mutual Educational and Cultural Exchange Act in 1961.

Taxable scholarships and grants after 1986. Under the new law, taxable scholarships and grants are treated as income for standard deduction purposes. A child eligible to be claimed as a dependent on his or her parent's return may use the standard deduction to offset the greater of $500 or earned income. For this purpose, scholarship or fellowship grants that are taxable under the new law may be treated as earned income.

RESTRICTIONS ON DEDUCTING CONSUMER INTEREST

Personal consumer interest after 1990 will no longer be deductible except for interest paid on home mortgages. Between 1987 and

1990, increasing amounts of consumer interest will not be deductible. In 1987, 65 percent of non-mortgage consumer interest will be deductible, and the remaining 35 percent not deductible; in 1988, 40 percent will be deductible, 60 percent not deductible; in 1989, 20 percent will be deductible, 80 percent not deductible; and in 1990, 10 percent will be deductible, 90 percent not deductible.

Consumer interest covers a broad range of interest expenses such as interest paid on tax deficiencies, installment contracts, educational loans, car loans, and credit card charges. The phaseout applies also to interest paid on debts incurred before 1987, but not to interest paid on a debt secured by your principal residence and on a second residence. Interest on mortgages on two residences is generally deductible. Further, as a homeowner, you may be able to avoid the phaseout rules by refinancing your home mortgage and using the loan proceeds to meet medical, educational, and other personal expenses. Interest on the mortgage debt is deductible provided tax law tests are met.

DEDUCTING INTEREST
ON RESIDENTIAL MORTGAGES

The tax rules for deducting home mortgage interest distinguish between mortgages made before, on, or after August 16, 1986. On mortgage loans secured on any residence made before August 17, 1986, interest paid on such loans is deductible and is not affected by the following law tests applied to mortgage loans made after August 16, 1986.

Whether interest is deductible on mortgage or refinancing after August 16, 1986, depends on:

(1) The cost basis of the residence including improvement costs;
(2) Existing mortgage debt, if any; and
(3) In some cases, how you use the loan proceeds.

If debt secured by the residence does not exceed cost basis plus improvements, the interest is deductible even if you use the loan proceeds to pay any type of consumer debt. If you want to borrow above cost basis plus improvements (but not over fair market value of the house), the interest is deductible if you use the loan proceeds to pay medical and educational expenses. If you use the proceeds for other purposes, the interest is treated as consumer interest.

EXAMPLES—

1. Cost basis in your principal residence is $100,000. Fair market value is $125,000. Your residence is subject to a purchase money mortgage of $60,000. You may refinance up to $100,000 (including the original $60,000 plus an additional $40,000). The interest in the new mortgage is deductible regardless of the type of consumer needs you apply the loan to.

2. You refinance for $110,000. To deduct interest on the $10,000 of the debt above $100,000 cost, you must show that the $10,000 proceeds are used to pay medical or educational expenses, or make improvements to the home.

Treat as cost basis the purchase price of the home. If you have deferred tax on the sale of a residence and bought a new home, cost basis for purposes of the interest rule is the cost of the new home, not the basis for tax deferral purposes. Cost basis includes improvement costs that under the law are treated as additions to basis. Basis is not reduced by depreciation as, for example, where you rent a second residence to tenants for a part of the year. The basis of an inherited residence is generally the value at the date if death of the decedent.

Qualified medical expenses are amounts paid for deductible medical care of the taxpayer, his or her spouse, and dependents. Qualified educational expenses are amounts paid for reasonable living expenses while away from home, and for any tuition and related expenses incurred that would qualify as scholarships for the taxpayer, his or her spouse or dependent, while a student at an educational organization. Thus, tuition expenses for primary, secondary, college, and graduate level education are generally qualified expenses. The qualified educational expenses or qualified medical expenses must be incurred within a reasonable period of time before or after the debt is incurred.

If you have more than two residences, you designate each year the second residence which secures the debt on which interest is claimed.

Cooperatives. In the case of housing cooperatives, debt secured by stock as a tenant-stockholder is treated as secured by a residence.

SALES TAXES ARE NOT DEDUCTIBLE AFTER 1986

Under pre-1987 law, you may claim itemized deductions for state and local taxes, income taxes, real estate property taxes, personal property taxes, and general sales taxes. Other state or local taxes and foreign taxes generally are deductible if incurred in a business or in an income-producing (investment) activity, including taxes incurred on a purchase or disposition of property. Starting in 1987, the itemized deduction is not allowed for state and local general sales taxes paid. The itemized deductions for state and local income, real property, and personal property taxes remain deductible.

Capitalization of sales tax. If you incur a sales tax on the purchase of business or investment property, you add the tax to the cost of the property. If the tax is incurred on a sale of such property, deduct the tax from the sales proceeds.

PRIZES AND AWARDS SUBJECT TO TAX

Under pre-1987 law, prizes and awards were generally taxable except for an award meeting these tests:

(1) It was in recognition of past accomplishments in religious, charitable, scientific, educational, artistic, literary, or civic fields.

(2) You did not enter the contest or proceeding. You were selected without any action on your part.

(3) You were not required as a condition of receiving the prize to perform substantial future services.

Starting in 1987, all prizes and awards are taxable unless you assign the prize or award to a government unit or tax-exempt charitable organization. You may not claim a charitable deduction for the assignment. You must make the assignment before you use a benefit from the award.

EMPLOYEE AWARDS MAY BE TAX-FREE UP TO A POINT

The new law sets limits on the type and amount of employee awards that may escape income tax. An achievement award, such as a watch, is tax free if given for length of service or safety achievements. The exclusion covers only tangible property, not cash or gift certificates. The tax-free exclusion does not apply when you receive an award for length of service during the first five years of employment or when you previously received such awards during the last five years, unless the prior award qualified as *de minimis* fringe benefits.

Safety achievement awards may not be made to managers, administrators, clerical workers, and other professional employees.

As a general rule, if your employer is allowed to deduct the cost of the award, you are not taxed. Therefore, it is up to your employer to tell you the tax consequences of the award. The deduction rules are as follows: There is a $400 limit on the deduction for safety and length of service (other than qualified plan awards) provided to the same employee during the taxable year. There is also a deduction ceiling of $1,600 for several qualified plan awards made to one employee whether for safety or length of service. A qualified plan award is an employee achievement award provided under an established written plan or program that does not discriminate in favor of highly compensated employees. Qualified plan treatment does not apply if the average cost per employee of all achievement awards made under all qualified award plans of the employer during the taxable year exceeds $400.

Part of the achievement award may be taxable if the cost of the award exceeds the allowable deduction. Taxable income is the larger of (1) the difference between cost of the award and the deduction or (2) the difference between the fair market value of the award and the deduction. For example, a watch given as a safety award that costs $600 is not a qualified plan award. The fair market value of the watch is $575. The deduction is limited to $400. The employee reports income of $200 (cost of $600 less the $400 deduction).

Certain gifts may also be tax free under fringe benefit rules not discussed in this book.

CASUALTY LOSS DEDUCTIONS FOR DEPOSITS LOST IN BANK FAILURES

You may claim a bad debt deduction for a loss of a bank deposit in the year there is no reasonable prospect of recovery from an insolvent or bankrupt bank or financial institution. The loss is claimed as a short-term capital loss unless the deposit was made in your business. Under a new law, you have another choice for taxable years after 1982. You may elect to take a casualty loss deduction for the year in which the loss can be reasonably estimated. The loss is subject to the 10 percent adjusted gross income floor for casualty losses. Choose the election that gives the greater tax reduction. The election is generally not allowed to stockholders or officers of the bank.

Once the casualty loss election is made, it is irrevocable and will apply to all other losses on deposits in the same financial institution.

INSURANCE CLAIMS
AND CASUALTY LOSSES

To avoid loss of insurance coverage or an increase in premium rates, you may decline to file an insurance claim for a loss. According to the IRS, your failure to make a claim prevents you from claiming a casualty loss deduction for the unreimbursed loss. Courts rejected the IRS position; however, Congress now favors the IRS by passing a law adopting the IRS rule. Starting in 1987, a nonbusiness casualty loss deduction may not be claimed for insured property unless you file a timely insurance claim. If you do not have insurance coverage, the rule, of course, does not apply.

INCREASED FLOOR
FOR MEDICAL EXPENSES

A wide range of expenses qualify as deductible medical expenses. However, you may not be able to claim the deduction because of a percentage floor. Starting in 1987, you may deduct only expenses exceeding 7.5 percent of your adjusted gross income. Before 1987, the floor was five percent. Married persons filing joint returns figure the 7.5 percent limit on combined adjusted gross income.

You include the cost of prescribed drugs and medical insurance premiums with other medical expenses subject to the 7.5 percent floor.

EXAMPLE—

Your adjusted gross income is $16,000. Your unreimbursed medical expenses were $900 for medical care, $187 for prescribed drugs and medicines, and $600 for medical insurance premiums. You deduct medical expenses of $487 figured this way:

Unreimbursed medical care	$900
Premiums	600
Drugs	187
Total	$1,687
Less: 7.5% of adjusted gross income	
(7.5% of $16,000)	1,200
Medical expense deduction	$ 487

In 1986, the AGI floor was five percent and your deduction
would have been $887 ($1,687 − $800).

HOW YOUR DEDUCTION IS REDUCED
BY THE 7.5 PERCENT FLOOR

If your adjusted gross income is	Your unreimbursed medical expenses are				
	$300	$500	$1,000	$2,000	$3,000
	You may deduct				
$5,000	0	125	625	1,625	2,625
$8,000	0	0	400	1,400	2,400
$10,000	0	0	250	1,250	2,250
$15,000	0	0	0	875	1,875
$20,000	0	0	0	500	1,500
$25,000	0	0	0	125	1,125
$30,000	0	0	0	0	750

Under the new law, handicapped individuals may treat as deductible medical expenses the cost of making structural changes to their
residence such as adding exit ramps, modifying doorways, installing
railings and support bars, and modifying hallways to accommodate

wheelchair passengers. Such improvements are considered deductible medical expenses even if they increase the value of the house.

REVISED ALIMONY RULES

The alimony rules for post-1986 agreements have been changed. A decree or agreement does not have to specifically state that alimony must end at death of payee-spouse, and the minimum payout and recapture period is reduced from six to three years as explained in the following paragraphs.

Planning Alimony. By taking tax rules into consideration, you, with your professional counselors, can arrange beforehand how the costs of a divorce are to be borne. Divorce and legal separations involve property settlements, alimony, and support payments. You may specifically state in the decree or agreement that the alimony is neither taxable to the payee-spouse (under IRC section 71) nor deductible by the payer-spouse (under section 215). Such a statement effectively disqualifies payments that otherwise would be taxable to the payee-spouse and deductible by the payer-spouse. The payee-spouse must attach a copy of the agreement that includes the statement to the tax return for the years in which it applies.

If you agree that one spouse is to pay deductible alimony and the other spouse is to report the alimony as income, these rules must be met:

(1) The alimony is paid under the decree of divorce or legal separation, written separation agreement or decree of support.

(2) The agreement must provide for cash payments. There is no minimum payout period for annual alimony payments of $15,000 or less. One payment of $15,000 can qualify as deductible and taxable alimony. There is, however, a minimum payout period of at least three years for annual alimony payments exceeding $15,000. The period can, of course, be longer than three years.

To avoid recapture of deductions of alimony exceeding $15,000, carefully plan or avoid schedules of declining payments. Recapture may occur where the annual payments of over $15,000 are scheduled and paid, but in the second or third year a reduced payment is made.

(3) In providing for the support of children, a specific allocation to their support or the setting of certain contingencies disqualifies payments as deductible and taxable alimony.

(4) Divorced and legally separated parties may not live in the same household. If they live in the same household, alimony payments are not deductible or taxable. However, there are these exceptions: A spouse who makes payments while preparing to leave the common residence may deduct payments made within one month before the departure. Also, where you are separated under a written agreement but not legally separated under a decree of divorce or separation maintenance, you may deduct alimony payments even if you both are members of the same household.

Cash Payments. Only payments of cash, checks, and money orders payable on demand qualify as taxable and deductible alimony. Providing services or transferring or providing property do not qualify. For example, you may not deduct as alimony your note, the assignment of a third-party note, or an annuity contract. Your cash payment to a third party for a spouse qualifies if made under the terms of a divorce decree or separation instrument. For example, you pay the rent, mortgage, tax or tuition liabilities of your former spouse. The payments qualify if made under the terms of the divorce or separation instrument. However, you may not deduct payments to maintain property owned by you but used by your spouse. For example, you pay the mortgage expenses, real estate taxes, and insurance premiums for a house which you own and in which your former spouse lives. You may not deduct those payments, even if required by a decree or agreement.

Recapture. If the alimony payments in the first year exceed the average payments made in the second and third year by more than $15,000, the excess amounts are recaptured in the third year. Further, where the payments in the second year exceed the payments in the third year by more than $15,000, the excess over $15,000 is recaptured. Recaptured amounts are reported by the payer-spouse as income and are deducted by the payee-spouse. The recapture rule is designed to prevent a person from making a deductible property settlement in the form of alimony.

Recapture is not required if either party dies or if the payee spouse remarries by the end of the calendar year which is two years after the payments begin and payments cease by reason of that event. Recapture does not apply to temporary support payments or payments which fluctuate as a result of a continuing liability to pay, for at least three years, a fixed portion or portions of income from the earnings of a business property or services.

EXAMPLES—

1. In the first year, Jones pays alimony of $50,000. In the second and third year, he makes no payments. In the third year, $35,000 is recaptured ($50,000 − 15,000) as income by Jones; his ex-spouse deducts $35,000.

2. In the first year, Smith pays alimony of $50,000; in the second year, $20,000; and in the third year, nothing. In the third year, $32,500 is recaptured as follows:

Recapture of second year payment:	
Payment	$20,000
Less	15,000
Recapture	$ 5,000
Recapture of first year payments:	
Average calculation	
Payment over the 2nd and 3rd years	$20,000
Less recapture in the 2nd year	5,000
	$15,000
Average ($15,000 divided by 2)	$7,500
Payment in first year	$50,000
Less average $ 7,500	
15,000	$22,500
Recapture	$27,500

Child support. Payments specified as or related to child support are not taxable or deductible as alimony. For example, if the amount paid is reduced upon an event related to the child (such as reaching specified age, leaving school, dying, or marrying), the payment is treated as child support to the extent of the reduction. If both alimony and child support are specified, any payment less than the total of the two amounts is first allocated to child support.

Figure the tax cost of each alternative; your lawyer will draft documents supporting your agreement. Understanding and settling the legal and tax consequences of marital disputes can avoid costly personal and tax disputes in the future.

SURVIVING SPOUSE EXCLUSION FOR INTEREST PAID ON INSURANCE INSTALLMENT REPEALED

Life insurance proceeds received because of the death of the insured are not generally subject to income tax. However, interest paid on proceeds left with the insurer is taxable but there may be an exception where a surviving spouse elects to receive installments rather than a lump sum. A surviving spouse does not pay tax on the first $1,000 of interest received each year, provided the deceased died before October 23, 1986. Under the new law when a person dies after October 22, 1986, interest paid on the insurance policy is taxable even though it is paid to a surviving spouse.

NEW WITHHOLDING ALLOWANCE FORMS MUST BE FILED BY EMPLOYEES

The IRS is revising its withholding tables based on the new tax rate schedules for 1987 and 1988. By October 1, 1987, you should file a revised Form W-4 with your employer to claim withholding allowances. Otherwise, withholdings from your pay will be based on one allowance if your prior Form W-4 indicates you are single or two allowances if your prior Form W-4 indicates you are married. Thus, to reduce withholdings based on extra dependency exemptions, such as for a child, you should file the new Form W-4.

ESTIMATED TAX

For years after 1986, the penalty for underpaying estimated tax through wage withholdings or quarterly installments will not apply if your payments equal the lesser of 90 percent of the current year's tax or 100 percent of the prior year's tax. Under prior law, the current year requirement was only 80 percent instead of 90 percent.

Waiver of 1986 penalty.   Some taxpayers may have based their 1986 estimated tax payments on tax-savings provisions such as the investment credit, which were repealed by the 1986 Tax Act. The Act provides that for periods before April 15, 1987, no penalty will be imposed for extra liability resulting from new law changes. For corporations, the waiver period ends March 16, 1987.

FAMILY INCOME PLANNING

The 1986 Tax Act discourages income splitting between parents and minor children under the age of 14, and the use of short-term trusts for shifting tax on trust income from the trust grantor to income beneficiaries. Starting in 1987, (1) income of over $1,000 earned on property transferred to children under the age of 14 is subject to tax at the parent's tax rate, and (2) the short-term trust (10-year) exception for grantor trusts has been repealed. However, income splitting opportunities remain available to parents for children 14 and over, and, to a limited extent, for children under 14.

Although the spread between tax brackets has been narrowed, income-splitting, whenever possible, continues as a tax-savings technique, although the amount of the future savings may not be as great as was possible under prior law.

HOW DEPENDENT CHILDREN ARE TAXED

Filing requirements. A 1987 return must be filed for a dependent child with gross income of at least $500 but there is this exception: If a dependent child has salary or other earned income but no investment income, a return does not have to be filed unless such earned income exceeds $2,540 in 1987. In 1988, a dependent child with only earned income will not have to file unless the earned income exceeds $3,000.

Gross income of $500 or less. A dependent child whose gross income (earned and unearned) is $500 or less will not be subject to tax after 1986. A dependent child may not claim a personal exemption on his or her tax return but is allowed to claim a $500 standard deduction.

Gross income over $500 but not over $1,000. If a dependent child's gross income is more than $500 but not over $1,000, taxable income is computed by reducing the income by the greater of (1) the standard deduction, or (2) allowable itemized deductions. The standard deduction equals the greater of $500 or earned income. Taxable income is subject to the child's tax bracket regardless of whether the child is age 14 or over.

Gross income exceeding $1,000.   If a dependent child has gross income over $1,000, the tax computation depends on whether he or she has reached age 14 by the end of the tax year and if under 14, whether income is earned income such as salary or unearned income such as investment or dividends. Under the 1986 Tax Act, **investment income exceeding $1,000** is taxed to a child under age 14 at his or her parent's top marginal rate. If the child has reached age 14 by the end of the year, all taxable income is taxed at the child's own tax bracket.

Dependent child age 14 or over.   After claiming the standard deduction or itemizing deductions, taxable income of a child age 14 or over (as of the end of the year) is taxed at the child's regular tax bracket. A dependent child's standard deduction equals the greater of (1) $500, or (2) earned income, up to the regular standard deduction limit.

EXAMPLE—

A dependent child is age 14 at the end of 1987. He has interest income of $1,200 and salary income of $750 from a part-time job. His standard deduction is $750, the greater of earned income or $500. No personal exemption may be claimed. Assuming the child may not itemize deductions, taxable income is $1,200 ($1,950 gross income - $750 standard deduction) which will be subject to the 11 percent bracket in 1987.

Taxable income	$1,200
Tax at 11 percent	$ 132

DETERMINING A TAX LIABILITY
OF A CHILD UNDER AGE 14

There are two steps in determining the income tax liability of a child under age 14.

Step 1. **Determining whether the child is liable to tax.** A child who is under 14 and who may be claimed as a dependent by his or her parent or other person is not allowed to claim a personal exemption, but is allowed to claim a standard deduction. The dependent child's standard deduction is the greater of $500 or the child's earned income from services, up to the regular standard deduction limit. If the child has both investment income and earned income, the standard deduction is allocated first to the investment income.

Step 2. **Determining income subject to parent's bracket.** The child's income may be taxed at two different rates: (1) the child's bracket and (2) the parent's top bracket. To determine income subject to the parent's tax bracket, the law introduces a tax term called net unearned income. This is gross investment income minus $500 minus the greater of (1) the $500 standard deduction limit for investment income or (2) the amount of allowable deductions directly connected with the production of the unearned income. Under this definition, net unearned income is not subject to the parent's tax bracket if the child does not have over $1,000 of unearned income. In 1988, the $500 amounts stated in the definition may be increased for inflation.

Do not confuse the computation of taxable income of step 1 with the tax bracket test of step 2 although both may be similar. The amount of allocated deductions in step 2 may be the same as in step 1.

EXAMPLES (In all the following examples, assume a child under the age 14)—

1. Child has interest income of $480 and no other income. The child has no income tax liability.

Interest income	$480
Less standard deduction	480

2. Child has interest and dividend income of $900 and no other income.

Tax liability test:

Total income	$900
Less standard deduction	500
Taxable income	$400

Bracket test:

Unearned income	$900
Less standard deduction	500
Balance	$400

The $400 is not subject to tax at parent's bracket as it does not exceed $500.

3. Child has dividend income of $1,300.

Tax liability test:

Dividend income	$1,300
Less standard deduction	500
Taxable income	$ 800

Bracket test:

Unearned income	$1,300
Less standard deduction	500
	800
Less $500	500
Taxed at parent's bracket	$ 300

4. The child has wages of $700 and $300 of interest income.
Tax liability test:

Total income	$1,000
Less standard deduction (up to wages)	700
Taxable income	$ 300

Tax bracket test:

Unearned income	300
Less standard deduction	$ 300

Parent's tax bracket does not apply; unearned income is offset by standard deduction.

5. Child has wages of $800 and dividends of $900.
Tax liability test:

Total income	$1,700
Less standard deduction (up to wages)	800
Taxable income	$ 900

Tax bracket test:

Unearned income	$ 900
Less standard deduction limit for unearned income	500
Balance	$ 400

As this is less than $500, it is not taxed at the parent's rate. The entire $400 is taxed at the child's rate. Further, as $500 of the $800 standard deduction is allocated to unearned income, the $300 balance offsets the child's wage income. Thus $500 of wages ($800 - $300) is also taxed at the child's rate in 1987.

6. Child has $300 salary and $1,200 dividends and interest. Itemized deductions of $400 connected to investment income after considering 2 percent AGI floor. Your child also has $400 of other itemized deductions.

Taxable income	$1,500
Less itemized deductions	800
Taxable income	$ 700

Tax bracket test:

Unearned income	$1,200

Less standard deduction limit	500
Balance	$ 700
Less $500	500
Taxed at parent's rate	$ 200

7. The child has $700 of salary income and $3,000 of investment income, and itemized deductions of $800 (net of the two percent floor) directly connected with the production of the investment income. The child has $200 of other deductions.

Tax liability test:

Total income	$3,700
Less itemized deductions	1,000
Subject to tax	$2,700

Tax bracket test:

Unearned income	$3,000
Deductions related to unearned income	800
	$2,200
Less $500	500
Taxed at parent's rate	$1,700

Thus, $500 of unearned income is taxed at the child's rate and $1,700 at the parent's rate. Of the child's $700 salary income, $200 is offset by the itemized deductions not connected with unearned income; the balance of $500 of salary income is taxed at the child's rate.

INCOME SPLITTING CAN SAVE TAXES

Each additional dollar of ordinary income you receive, such as interest, dividends, and rent, is taxed in your highest bracket. If, under the 1986 Tax Act, you can deflect income to a lower tax bracket of a child or other dependent relative, he or she will pay a smaller tax on the income than you would pay. This tax-saving technique, known as income splitting, allows more after-tax income to remain within the family.

To split income, you must do more than make gifts of income. You must transfer the actual property from which the income is produced. For example, you do not avoid tax on interest by instructing your savings bank to credit interest to your children's account. Unless you actually transfer the complete ownership of the account to your children, the interest is earned on money owned by you and must be reported by you. The same holds true with dividends, rents, and other forms of income. Unless you transfer the property providing the income, the income will be taxed to you.

You may not split earned income; income resulting from your services is taxed to you. You may not avoid this result by setting up trusts to receive your earned income.

As family income planning generally requires the transfer of property, you must consider possible gift tax liability. However, gift tax liability may be avoided by making gifts within the annual exclusion of $10,000 (or $20,000 for joint gifts). To each donee, you may give annually up to $10,000 tax free; further, if your spouse joins in the gift, you may give annually tax free to each donee up to $20,000. Thus, if you (with your spouse's consent) make annual gifts to four persons, you could give away without gift tax up to $80,000 (4 × $20,000 exclusion). Gifts over this exclusion may also avoid tax after applying the unified gift and estate tax credit.

If you make an interest-free or low-interest loan to a family member, you may be subject to income tax as well as gift tax.

Custodian accounts for children.   Custodian accounts set up in a bank, mutal fund, or brokerage firm can achieve income splitting. Trust accounts which are considered revocable under state law are ineffective in splitting interest income.

Purchase of securities through custodian accounts provides a practical method for making a gift of securities to a minor child, eliminating the need for a trust. The mechanics of opening a custodian account are simple. An adult opens a stock account for a minor child at a broker's office. The adult registers the securities in the name of the custodian for the benefit of the child. The custodian may be a parent, a child's guardian, grandparent, brother or sister, uncle or aunt. In some states, the custodian may be any adult or a bank or trust company. The custodian has the right to sell securities in the account, collect sales proceeds and investment income, and use them for the child's benefit or reinvestment.

There are limitations placed on custodians. They may not take proceeds from the sale of an investment or income from an investment to buy additional securities on margin. While they should prudently seek reasonable income and capital preservation, they generally are not liable for losses unless the losses result from bad faith, intentional wrongdoing, or gross negligence.

When the minor reaches majority (depending on state law), property in the custodian account is turned over to the child. No formal accounting is required. The child, now an adult, may sign a simple release freeing the custodian from any liability. But reaching the age of majority, the child may require a formal accounting if there are any doubts as to the propriety of the custodian's actions while acting as custodian. For this reason and also for tax record-keeping purposes, a separate bank account should be opened in which are deposited proceeds pending reinvestment on behalf of the child. Such an account will furnish a convient record of sales proceeds, investment income, and reinvestment of the same.

Although custodian accounts may be opened anywhere in the United States, the rules governing the account may vary from state to state. The differences between the laws of the states generally do not affect federal tax consequences.

Income tax treatment. Income from a custodian account is taxable to the child as long as it is not used by the parent who set up the account to pay for the child's support. Tax-exempt income from a custodian account is not taxable to the parent even when used for child support. Starting in 1987, taxable income from a custodian account may be taxable at the parent's tax rate if the child is under 14. This rule does not apply to children 14 or over.

Gift tax treatment. When setting up a custodian account, you may have to pay a gift tax. A transfer of cash or securities to a custodian account is a gift. But you are not subject to a gift tax if you properly plan the cash contributions or purchase of securities for your child's accounts. You may make gifts up to $10,000 to one person, which is shielded from gift tax by the annual exclusion. The exclusion applies each year to each person to whom you make a gift. If your spouse consents to join with you in the gift, you may give annually tax free up to $20,000 to each person.

If the custodian account is set up at the end of December, another tax-free transfer of $20,000 may be made in the first days of January of the following year. In this way, a total of $40,000 is shifted within the two-month period.

Estate tax treatment.   The value of a custodian account will be taxed in your estate if you die while acting as custodian of an account before the child reaches majority. However, you may avoid the problem by naming someone other than yourself as custodian. If you should decide to act as custodian, taking the risk that the account will be taxed in your estate, remember no estate tax is incurred if the tax on your estate is offset by the estate tax credit.

If you act as custodian and decide to terminate the custodianship, care should be taken to formally close the account. Otherwise, if you die while retaining power over the account, the IRS may try to tax the account in your estate.

Other types of investments for children.   A minor generally lacks the ability to manage property. Yet, if you exercise control over the property you give to him, the gift may not be recognized for purposes of shifting income. You might appoint a fiduciary for the child, but this step may be costly. Alternatively you might select property which does not require management and which can be transferred by the minor. For example—

(1) Bonds may be purchased and registered in a minor's name and coupons or the proceeds on a sale or maturity of bonds may be cashed or deposited in a minor's name.

(2) Insurance companies will write policies on the lives of minors and recongnize their ownership of policies covering the lives of others. Depending on the age of the minor, state law, and company practice, it may be necessary to appoint a guardian for the purpose of cashing in or borrowing on insurance policies given to a minor. A gift of a life insurance policy or an annuity will usually qualify as a gift of a present interest in property for the annual gift tax exclusion.

(3) Mutual fund shares, such as money market funds, may be purchased and registered in the name of a minor. The problem of management and sale for reinvestment is minimized because the investment trust itself provides continuous supervision. Changes in the underlying investments of the fund are made without reference to the minor. Most funds provide for automatic reinvestment of dividends in additional shares.

U.S. Savings Bonds (EE) may be cashed in for their purchase price plus an increase in their value. The increase over cost is taxable as interest. The reporting of this interest may be deferred until the year the bond is cashed in or matures, whichever is earlier. Because of this deferral election, savings bonds may be considered for accumulating an educational fund for children. If the children are under age 14, deferring tax on the interest does not subject the interest to tax at the parent's tax bracket.

TAX SAVINGS
FOR 10-YEAR TRUSTS
CURTAILED

Ten-year (Clifford) trusts have been widely used to shift income to relatives in lower tax brackets. Where a trust met the ten-year exception, trust income was taxed to the beneficiary, usually a minor child. Another type of trust used for income splitting was the spousal remainder trust setup for less than ten years. It allowed income shifting to a child beneficiary when the trust property went to the grantor's spouse after the trust period ends.

Under the new law, both types of trust may no longer be used to shift income to the income beneficiary. The ten-year exemption for grantor trusts is repealed. The grantor of a grantor trust is taxed on the income of the trust. A trust is treated as a grantor trust where the grantor has a reversionary interest (at the time of the transfer) of more than five percent of the value of the property transferred to the trust. Spousal remainder trusts are neutralized as tax saving techniques by a new law treating the grantor as holding a reversionary interest held by his spouse if the spouse is living with the grantor.

The new rules apply to trust transfers made after March 1, 1986. An exception applies to the ten-year trust created pursuant to a binding property settlement entered into before March 2, 1986, which required the taxpayer to establish a grantor trust.

Status of prior ten-year trusts.   Trusts created before the effective date continue to shift income to the income beneficiary. However, tax-savings are nullified for trust beneficiaries under the age of 14. Unearned income over $1,000 of a child under 14 is taxed to the child at the top marginal rate of the parents.

Pre-March 1, 1986, ten-year trusts will continue to shift income and provide tax savings to trust beneficiaries 14 or over.

Tax rates for trusts and estates.   For taxable years beginning in 1987, a five-tier rate schedule applies with rates of 11, 15, 28, 35, or 38.5 percent. The top rate of 38.5 percent applies to taxable income over $15,150. For taxable years beginning after December 31, 1987, the first $5,000 of taxable income of a trust or estate will be taxed at a 15 percent rate, with excess income taxed at 28 percent. The benefit of the 15 percent bracket will be phased out between $13,000 and $26,000 of taxable income.

INVESTMENTS

LONG-TERM CAPITAL GAIN
TAXED AS ORDINARY INCOME

The new law repeals the 60 percent deduction for long-term capital gains for taxable years beginning after 1986 but not the distinction between short-term and long-term capital gains and losses.

Repeal of capital gain deduction. Under pre-1986 law, the capital gain deduction allowed long-term capital gain to be taxed at low income tax rates. Before its repeal, the capital gain deduction was 60 percent so that only 40 percent of your net long-term capital gains was taxable along with your other taxable income. Thus, if you were in the 50 percent bracket, the effective tax rate on long-term capital gain was 20 percent (40% x 50%).

EXAMPLES—

1. In 1986, you had salary income of $50,000, long-term capital gain income of $50,000, and excess itemized deductions of $10,000. You file a joint return.

Salary income		$50,000
Long-term capital gain	$50,000	
Less: Capital gain deduction	30,000	20,000
Adjusted gross income		$70,000
Less: Excess itemized deductions	10,000	
Exemption	2,160	12,160
Taxable Income		$57,840

2. Same facts as above in 1987, except all of your capital gains are subject to tax.

Salary income		$50,000
Capital gain		50,000
		$100,000
Less Itemized deduction	$13,760	
Exemption	3,800	17,560
Taxable Income		$ 82,440

In 1987, income of $82,440 falls in the 35 percent bracket. However, your long-term capital gain will be subject to only a top tax of 28 percent.

Retention of capital gain distinctions.   In 1987, you will still follow the short- and long-term holding period rules. Gains and losses on sales of capital assets held for six months or less are short-term, and gains and losses on sale of capital assets held for more than six months are long-term. Further, as in the past, in each group, gains and losses will be offset. In the long-term group, you will offset long-term gains and losses from each other. In the short-term group, you will offset short-term gains and losses from each other. Depending upon all your transactions in 1987, you will have one of these results:

(1) **Net long-term gain.** All of your net long-term gain is subject to tax at ordinary income rates of not more than 28 percent.

EXAMPLE—

You sell four lots of securities for long-term profit of $12,000. $12,000 is added to your other income.

(2) **Net long-term loss.** You may deduct your long-term loss from other income up to a maximum deduction of $3,000. The loss when applied to other income is not reduced by 50 percent as under pre-1987 law.

EXAMPLE—

Your only capital asset transaction is a sale of securities held long term. You realize a loss of $7,000. Your other income from salary, dividends, and interest is $28,000. You deduct $3,000 from your other income of $28,000. You also have a carryover loss of $4,000 to 1988 and later years.

(3) **Net short-term gain.** Add the full amount of short-term gain to your other income. Short-term gain is fully taxed as ordinary income.

EXAMPLE—

Your only capital asset transaction is a sale of stock held for five months. You realize a profit of $8,000 which is added to your ordinary income.

(4) **Net short-term loss.** You deduct this loss from your other income up to $3,000. If the loss exceeds your ordinary income, or is more than $3,000, the unused loss is carried over as a short-term loss to 1988 and later years.

(5) **Net long-term gain and net short-term gain.** All of net long-term gain and net short-term gain is added to your other income. However, long-term gain is not taxed at more than 28 percent.

(6) **Net long-term gain and net short-term loss.** Deduct the short-term loss from the net long-term gain. If the net short-term loss exceeds the net long-term gain, the remaining loss is deductible from other income up to $3,000. After this deduction from ordinary income, any remaining loss is carried over to later years. If the long-term gain exceeds the short-term loss, the remaining long-term gain is added to other income.

EXAMPLE—

You sell two lots of securities held for two years at a profit of $9,000. You also sell one lot of securities held for three months at a loss of $10,000. Combining both the loss and the gain leaves a short-term capital loss of $1,000, which may be deducted from ordinary income. If the short-term loss were $4,000, a net long-term capital gain of $5,000 ($9,000 − $4,000) would have resulted, and would be added to your other income and subject to a tax rate not exceeding 28 percent.

(7) **Net short-term gain and net long-term loss.** Deduct the long-term loss from the short-term gain. If the gain exceeds the loss, add the full amount of the remaining gain to your other income. If the loss exceeds the gain, the remaining long-term loss is deductible up to $3,000 of ordinary income (see (2) above).

EXAMPLE—

You realize a net short-term gain of $3,000 and net long-term loss of $4,000. By combining both figures, you get a net loss of $1,000, deductible from ordinary income. If the long-term loss were $2,500, net short-term gain of $500 would be added to your ordinary income.

(8) **Net long-term loss and net short-term loss.** The losses reduce up to $3,000 of ordinary income in this order: First apply the short-term loss, then the long-term loss.

Capital loss carryovers. You have a capital loss carryover when the ordinary income ceiling of up to $3,000 prevents you from deducting the full amount of your net capital loss. You have an unlimited period of time to deduct the loss from future gains.

ALTERNATIVE MINIMUM TAX INCREASES

The alternative minimum tax (AMT) is designed to recoup tax benefits that have reduced or eliminated your regular income tax. AMT is imposed if it exceeds your regular income tax or you have no tax liability after claiming certain tax deductions or credits. You may incur an AMT if you have deductions for accelerated and ACRS depreciation, percentage depletion, and intangible drilling and development costs.

Even when you do not have the above preference items, you may incur an AMT if you have substantial itemized deductions that are not deductible for AMT purposes. For AMT purposes, state and local income taxes are not deductible and there is a limited interest deduction.

Under the law, starting in 1987, the AMT rate is 21 percent. In 1986, the rate was 20 percent.

You compute your AMT after you have figured your regular tax on Form 1040. You figure AMT liability on Form 6251, which is attached to Form 1040.

The starting point for computing AMT is adjusted gross income.

On Form 6251, adjusted gross income is increased by tax preference items and reduced by certain itemized deductions. State and local taxes are not deductible for AMT purposes. If you have a net operating loss, the loss for AMT purposes is not included in adjusted gross income. The loss is reduced before it is deductible from AMT income.

AMT income may be reduced further by one of the following exemptions: $40,000 on joint returns, $30,000 for unmarried individuals, and $20,000 for married persons filing separately. However, starting with 1987 tax years, the exemption is reduced by 25 cents for each $1 that alternative minimum taxable income exceeds these amounts: $150,000 for joint filers, $112,500 for individuals, and $75,000 for married couples filing separately. The effect of the exemption phaseout is to apply roughly a 26 percent tax for those with income in the phaseout range.

Under the new law, passive losses from tax shelters and other investments plus certain passive farming losses may not be used to reduce alternative minimum taxable income. The full passive loss is denied for AMT purposes although for purposes of the regular income tax, the limits on passive losses will be phased in over five years. Finally, after 1986, the untaxed appreciation on charitable contributions of property and interest paid on tax-exempt bonds for non-essential private functions issued after August 7, 1986, will be AMT preference items.

If you expect to reduce substantially your regular tax through tax shelter benefits treated as AMT tax preference items, make sure to project your possible AMT liability. This may involve complicated calculations and it may be advisable to have an experienced accountant help you. If you are close to or within the range of the AMT tax, the following steps can avoid or soften the impact of the tax:

> Defer deductible expense items to a later year in which your income will be subject to tax rates exceeding 21 percent. Consider deferring payment of charitable donations, interest, and medical expenses. You will get a larger tax benefit from the deductions in the later year. In the case of

certain realty or equipment purchases, consider an election to capitalize taxes and carry charges. Also, do not elect first-year expensing of business equipment.

Defer if possible the exercise of an incentive stock option to a later year. The bargain element of incentive stock option is a preference item subject to AMT. This is the difference between the option price and the fair market price of the stock on the date of exercise. If you exercise the option and it is subject to AMT along with other tax shelter preferences, you may find yourself with an unexpected liability and short of liquid funds to meet your tax liability.

Accelerating income.   If you find that you will be subject to AMT in a current year, you may want to subject additional income in that year to the AMT tax rate. In such a case, consider accelerating the receipt of income to that year. If you are in business, you might ask for earlier payments from customers or clients. If you control a small corporation, you might prepay salary or pay larger bonuses. But here be careful not to run afoul of reasonable compensation rules. You might also consider paying dividends. If you hold savings certificates with a six-month maturity in a later year, you might consider an early redemption to the current year. But here weigh the penalty cost of an early forfeiture. Similarly you might make an early sale of U.S. Treasury Bills to the current year.

If you are certain that you will be subject to AMT you may consider switching some tax-free investments into taxable investments which will give a higher after-tax return after the 21 percent AMT tax.

NEW RESTRICTIONS ON
TAX-EXEMPT BONDS

In buying state or local bonds, check the prospectus for the issue date of the bond. The 1986 Tax Act provides different tax treatment for bonds issued after August 7, 1986. Under the 1986 Tax Act, bonds fall within these classes:

(1) **"Public-purpose" bonds.**These include bonds issued directly by state or local governments or their agencies to meet essential government functions, such as highway construction and school financing. These bonds are generally tax-exempt.

(2) **"Nongovernmental purpose" bonds.** These include bonds issued to finance qualifying housing and student loans. There are limits on the amount of nongovernmental-purpose bonds an authority may issue. Interest on bonds issued after August 7, 1986, are tax-free for regular income tax purposes but are "preference items" to be added to taxable income if you are subject to alternative minimum tax. Because of the AMT factor, a nongovernment purpose bond may pay slightly more interest than public-purpose bonds. These may be a good investment if you are not subject to AMT tax or your AMT liability is not substantial. Bonds issued before August 8, 1986, are not affected by the above rules.

(3) **"Taxable" municipals.** These are bonds issued after August 31, 1986, for nonessential purposes, such as building a sports stadium. They are subject to federal income tax but may be exempt from state and local taxes in the states in which they are issued.

Tax-saving opportunity.   Tax exempt obligations are one of the few qualified tax shelter investments allowed by law. Although interest rates on tax-exempt bonds are generally lower than those of corporate bonds or Treasury bills and bonds of comparable safety and quality, in your tax bracket, the difference in interest rates may be more than offset by the tax that would be incurred on the higher interest.

To compare the interest return of a tax-exempt with that of a taxable bond, figure the taxable return that is equivalent to the tax-free yield of the tax-exempt. This amount depends on your tax bracket. For example, for a person in 1987 whose income was subject to a tax rate of 38.5 percent, a municipal bond yielding seven percent was the equivalent of a taxable yield of 11.4 percent. The following table shows the amount a taxable bond would have to earn to equal the tax-exempt bond, according to the investor's income tax bracket.

* A tax-exempt yield of

If top income tax rate is:	6%	7%	8%	9%	10%	11%
		is the equivalent of these taxable yields:				
28%	8.3	9.7	11.1	12.5	13.9	15.3
35%	9.2	10.8	12.3	13.8	15.4	16.9
38.5%	9.7	11.4	13.0	14.6	16.3	17.9

* Exemption from the tax of the state issuing the bond will increase the yield.

To lock in high rates, you may have to invest in a long-term bond. However, consider these drawbacks: You may not want to tie up your capital long term. There is the possibility that a future increase in interest rates may reduce the value of your investment if you should need the principal before maturity.

Most municipal bonds issued before July 1, 1983, except for housing issues, are in the form of bearer bonds; the owners are not identified and interest coupons are cashed as they come due. However, state and municipal bonds issued after June 30, 1983, with a maturity of more than one year, as well as obligations of the federal government and its agencies, are in registered form. Principal and interest is transferable only through an entry on the books of the issuer. The Treasury plans a system for registering obligations now held in street name.

INVESTMENT INTEREST DEDUCTIONS LIMITATIONS

Under pre-1987 law, deductions for interest paid on debt to buy or carry investment property were restricted. Each year, you could deduct interest up to $10,000 a year plus net investment income. Starting in 1987, the deduction will be subject to stricter restrictions. Generally, investment interest may offset only net investment income. However, a declining percentage of the $10,000 allowance will be allowed in 1987 through 1990.

What is investment interest? It is all interest (except consumer interest and qualified residence interest) on debt not incurred in your active trade or business. For example, if you borrow to buy securities, the interest you pay is investment interest. If you borrow to invest in a business in which you do not materially participate, interest expenses allocated to the business activity is investment interest provided the activity is not a "passive activity" under the passive loss rule. For example, interest expenses allocated to a working interest in oil or gas property, which by law is not treated as a passive activity, would be considered investment interest if you do not materially participate in the oil or gas venture. If your business activity is within the passive activity rule, the interest expense is treated as investment interest to the extent the interest is allocated to "portfolio" income which is interest, dividends, royalty or annuity income on the investment of business funds, rather than income derived directly from business operations. Further, interest allocated to rental real estate in which you actively participate is not investment interest.

What is net investment income? Net investment income, which may be offset by investment interest, is investment income reduced by expenses that are directly connected with the production of investment income.

The following are examples of investment income:

(1) Interest, dividends, rents, and royalties.
(2) Gain from the disposition of investment property.
(3) Portfolio income under the passive loss rules.
(4) Income from a business in which you do not materially participate if the activity is not considered passive activity under the passive loss rule.

Property subject to a net lease is not treated as investment property because it is treated as a passive activity under the passive loss rule. Income from rental real estate in which you actively participate is not included in investment income.

In figuring deductible investment expenses, the two percent adjusted gross income floor is considered. For example, you pay investment expenses for investment counseling of $2,000. You may treat only the excess of the expense over the floor as an investment expense.

Phaseout of $10,000 allowance. If investment interest exceeds net investment income by more than $10,000, no deduction may be claimed for the excess over $10,000. However, between 1987 and 1990, a percentage of the first $10,000 of excess investment interest (over net investment income) is deductible. In 1987, 65 percent of the $10,000 allowance is deductible; 40 percent in 1988; 20 percent in 1989; and 10 percent in 1990. After 1990, no deduction is allowed for investment interest that exceeds net investment income. To the extent it is disallowed under the phaseout, interest may be carried over and applied against investment income of a later year if expenses in such year are less than investment income in such a year.

EXAMPLE—

In 1987, you have $15,000 of investment interest in excess of investment income. $5,000 of the interest exceeding the allowance is not deductible. However, you may deduct 65 percent of the interest covered by the $10,000 allowance or $6,500 ($10,000 x 65%). If you have a passive loss that is allowed under the special phase-in rule applied to passive losses, the amount of that loss also reduces investment income.

AMORTIZING BOND PREMIUM

Bond premium is the extra amount paid for a bond in excess of its par value. You may elect to amortize bond premium or leave the basis of the bond unchanged. Amortizing is usually advisable.

Under the new law, if you make an election to amortize you must use a method of amortization fixed by law called constant yield method. The method of calculation is explained by Treasury regulations and generally applies to bonds issued after September 27, 1985. Under prior law, you were allowed to deduct the premium under the straight-line method.

If you do not amortize the premium, you will realize a capital loss when the bond is redeemed at par or you sell it for less than you paid for it. For example, you buy a $1,000 corporate bond for $1,150. You do not amortize the premium of $150. When the bond is redeemed at par, you will realize a long-term loss of $150. The premium is treated as part of the basis of the bond.

Redemption proceeds	$1,000
Cost basis	1,150
Loss	($ 150)

Why is amortizing the premium annually usually the advisable method? You get a current deduction against ordinary income if you claim itemized deductions. You also reduce the cost basis of the bond by the amount of the premium taken as a deduction. If you hold the bond to maturity, the entire premium is amortized and you have neither gain nor loss on redemption of the bond. If you sell the bond at a gain (selling price exceeds your basis for the bond), you realize long-term capital gain if you hold the bond long term. A sale of the bond for less than its adjusted basis gives a capital loss.

If you choose to amortize, the election applies to all bonds owned by you at the beginning of the first year you make the choice and to all bonds acquired thereafter. You make an election to amortize by taking the deduction on your tax return in the first year you decide to amortize the bond premium. If you file your tax return without claiming the deduction, you may not change your mind and make the election by filing an amended return or refund claim.

Premium paid on bonds with original issue discount.   The premium may be amortized on the straight-line method over the remaining term of the bond bought on or before July 18, 1984. For bonds bought after July 18, 1984, the premium is amortized by reducing original issue discount by a fraction. The numerator of the fraction is the premium; the denominator is the amount of the original issue discount still remaining on the bond at the time of purchase.

NOTE: You may not take a deduction for the amortization of premium paid on a tax-exempt bond. When you dispose of the bond, you amortize the premium for the period you held the bond and reduce the basis of the bond by the amortized amount.

STRADDLES: MARK-TO-MARKET RULE AND QUALIFIED COVERED CALLS

The new law retains the mark-to-market rules for regulated futures contracts, certain listed options, and forward contracts traded in the interbank market. These are marked to market at the close of the taxable year, with gain taxed as 60 percent long-term and 40 percent short-term for a maximum tax rate of 32 percent. The mark-to-market rules do not generally apply to hedging transactions, except in the case of certain syndicates.

Year-end rule for qualified covered calls. A qualified covered call is an option which an investor-stockholder grants on publicly traded stock. It is not treated as part of a straddle. Under prior law, this call exception was not allowed to an investor who failed to hold stock for 30 days after the related call option was sold at a loss, and gain on sale of the stock was reported in the next year. In such a case, the loss deduction was deferred. The same straddle loss-deferral rule will also apply after 1986 where the stock is sold at a loss, and gain on the related option held less than 30 days is reported in the next year.

TAX SHELTERS

TAX SHELTER LOSSES RESTRICTED

Under pre-1987 law, the motivating force behind tax shelter investment was the chance to use substantial deductions generated from the venture to offset salary and other investment income such as dividends and interest. Starting in 1987, this basic tax saving technique is no longer effective. You may not deduct from other income (salary, interest, dividends, annuity, self-employment income, etc.) losses from tax shelters and any business in which you do not materially participate. Such losses may offset only income from passive activities. Similarly, tax credits from passive activities are likewise limited to the tax allocable to income from passive activities. Disallowed losses and credits are suspended and carried forward to the next taxable year, where they may be used only against passive income. Any remaining suspended loss may be deducted when you sell your interest. However, a suspended credit may not be claimed in the year you sell your interest.

The passive loss restrictions apply to all passive investments (unless excepted by law)—even to your rental of an apartment in a two-family house that you own and to a business in which you invest money but do not manage, for example, you invest in a business operated by your children.

Income received for the performance of personal services in a passive activity is not treated as income from a passive activity. For example, as a limited partner, if you are paid for performing services for the partnership, the payments may not be offset by passive losses from the partnership or from any other passive activity.

Important: Otherwise disallowable losses of tax shelters and other passive interests acquired before October 23, 1986, may qualify for partial deductions during a five-year phase-out period.

RENTING IS A PASSIVE ACTIVITY

The ownership of rental property is treated as a passive activity, regardless of whether or not you participate in operating the property. You may not avoid the passive loss restriction by showing that you manage the property.

Rental activities—where payments are principally for the use of property—are presumed by law to be a passive activity. This passive loss restriction applies to rentals of apartments (whether long- or short-term) and long-term rentals of office equipment, automobiles, and/or a vessel under a bare-boat charter or a plane under a dry lease (no pilot or captain and no fuel) and net-leased property. A property is under a net-lease if the deductions (other than rents and reimbursed amounts) are less than 15 percent of rental income or where the lessor is guaranteed a specific return or is guaranteed against loss of income. Rental activities, however, do not include short-term car rentals and rentals of hotel rooms or similar space to transients.

Real estate dealers are generally not treated as engaging in a passive activity.

Providing incidental services, such as a laundry room in an apartment building, is considered part of the rental activity.

REAL ESTATE RENTALS
GET LIMITED LOSS ALLOWANCE

You may take advantage of a limited break if you perform some management role. You may deduct up to $25,000 of your loss to offset income from any source.

A trust may not qualify for the $25,000 allowance. Thus you cannot circumvent the $25,000 ceiling, or multiply the number of $25,000 allowances, simply by transferring various rental real properties to one or more trusts.

If you are married but live apart from your spouse and file a separate return, the $25,000 allowance, and the adjusted gross income phase-out range is reduced by 50 percent. If you file separately and at any time during the taxable year live with your spouse, no allowance at all may be claimed.

The limited allowance is phased out when your adjusted gross income is over $100,000. For every dollar of income over

$100,000, the loss allowance is reduced by 50 cents. When your income reaches $150,000, there is no allowance.

If AGI is	Loss Allowance is
up to $100,000	$25,000
110,000	20,000
120,000	15,000
130,000	10,000
140,000	5,000
150,000 or more	-0-

Qualifying for the allowance.   You must meet an active-participation test. Having an agent manage your property does not prevent you from meeting the test. You may meet the test by showing that you or your spouse participate in decisions, such as selecting tenants, setting rental terms and reviewing expenses. You must also have at least a 10 percent interest in the property. By law, limited partners are not considered active participants and thus do not qualify for the allowance.

EXAMPLE—

You rent out an apartment in a two-family house which you own and live in. In a year that your expenses exceeded your rental income, and your AGI is under $100,000, you may deduct up to $25,000 of the loss.

Mortgage interest on a principal residence or second residence is not subject to the passive loss rule when you rent out the residence.

Figuring the $25,000 allowance.   First match income and loss from all of your rental real estate activities in which you actively participate. A net loss from these activities is then applied to net passive income (if any) from other activities to determine the $25,000 allowance.

EXAMPLE—

You have $25,000 of losses from a rental real estate activity in which you actively participate. You also actively participate in another rental real estate activity, from which you had a $25,000 gain.

There is no net loss from rental estate activities in which you actively participate and no $25,000 allowance is permitted.

The allowance may not be used against carryover losses from prior taxable years when you were not an active participant.

Adjusted gross income, for purposes of the phase-out is figured without considering IRA contributions and taxable social security benefits.

In the case of an estate of a deceased taxpayer who owned an interest in a rental real estate activity in which he actively participated, the estate is deemed to actively participate for the two years following the death of the taxpayer.

MATERIAL PARTICIPATION TEST FOR BUSINESSES OTHER THAN RENTAL REAL ESTATE

If you do not "materially participate" in a business (other than rental real estate), your share of losses from the business is tainted as a passive loss. As such, you may not deduct the loss from your other income. Material participation generally requires involvement in daily business operations. Your services must be regular, continuous, and substantial. If you are a limited partner, you do not by law meet the material participation test.

In determining material participation, committee reports suggest this approach:

(1) **Is the activity your principal business?** For example, if your main business is farming, you are more likely to materially participate in a farm than an executive who invests in a farm venture. By law, a farmer who materially participates in a farm and retires retains that status after retirement, as does the spouse.

(2) **Do you live near the activity?** You are more likely to be actively involved in a business close to your home.

(3) What is your knowledge and experience in the business? A full-time manager of a business including several business activities may be considered to be materially participating in those activities although he is involved in management rather than operations. You are likely to be materially participating in an activity, if you do everything required to be done to conduct the activity, even though the actual amount of work to be done to conduct the activity is low in comparison to other activities.

In farming, regular and continuous decision-making may be considered in these areas:

(1) Crop rotation, selection, and pricing;
(2) the incursion of embryo transplant or breeding expenses;
(3) the purchase, sale, and leasing of capital items, such as cropland, animals, machinery, and equipment;
(4) breeding and mating decisions; and
(5) the selection of herd or crop managers who then act for you, rather than as paid advisors directing your decisions.

The material-participation rule applies whether you (or your spouse) own an interest as a proprietor, general partner, or S corporation shareholder. For a personal service corporation or a closely held C corporation to meet the test, one or more shareholders who own 50 percent or more of the stock must materially participate in the activity.

An alternative test applies to a closely held C corporation. The material participation rule is met if:

(1) At least one full-time employee works full time and year-round in the active management of the activity;
(2) At least three employees, other than owners, work full-time in the activity for the entire year; and
(3) Business deductions of the activity exceed 15 percent of its gross income.

Research and experimentation deductions. If you have an interest in a venture involving research and experimentation, and you do not materially participate in the activity, losses (including the research and experimentation expenditures) are subject to the passive loss rules.

PARTIAL DEDUCTIONS FOR
PRE-OCTOBER 23, 1986, INVESTMENTS

The full effect of the passive loss rule will not apply until 1991 for investments you held on October 22, 1986, the date the 1986 Tax Act was enacted.

During a five-year period, passive losses and credits are deductible at this rate.

In	Rate
1987	65%
1988	40
1989	20
1990	10

After 1991, deductions or credits are allowable only if they meet the new passive loss rules.

To take advantage of the phase-in, your investment interests in passive activities must have been acquired on or before October 22, 1986. Interests acquired after that date are not eligible for the phase-in and are fully subject to the passive loss rule.

A contractual obligation to purchase an interest in a passive activity binding on October 22, 1986, may be treated as an acquisition of the interest in the activity. A binding contract qualifies even if your obligation to acquire an interest is subject to contingencies, provided the contingencies are beyond your control. Thus, if you signed on or before October 22, 1986, a subscription agreement to buy a limited partnership interest contingent upon the agreement of other purchasers to acquire interests in the limited partnership amounting to a particular total, then if the contingency is satisfied, you are eligible for the phase-in rule. On the other hand, a conditional obligation to purchase or one subject to contingencies within your control does not qualify.

Where, after October 22, 1986, you contribute additional capital to the activity, you still qualify in full for the phase-in to the extent that your percentage ownership interest does not change as a result of the contribution. However, if your ownership interest is increased after October 22, 1986, then that part of your interest attributable to the increase does not qualify for the phase-in.

EXAMPLES—

1. After October 22, 1986, you increase your ownership interest in a partnership from 25 percent to 50 percent, then only the losses attributable to the 25 percent interest qualify for the phase-in relief. Phase-in relief applies only with respect to the percentage interest held by the taxpayer at all times after the date of enactment.

2. After October 22, 1986, you reduce your interest from 50 percent to 25 percent, and later purchase additional interests restoring your share to 50 percent, then only the 25 percent share held throughout qualifies for phase-in relief.

To qualify for the phase-in relief, the interest must be in an activity that has commenced by October 22, 1986. For example, a rental activity has commenced when the rental property has been placed in service in the activity. When the venture in which you own an interest liquidates or disposes of one activity and begins another after October 22, 1986, the new activity does not qualify. In the case of a house purchased for personal use but converted to rental use, the residence must be held out for rental by October 22, 1986.

Where the activity did not commence by October 22, 1986, phase-in treatment may apply if the venture has entered into a binding contract effective on or before August 16, 1986, to acquire the assets used to conduct the activity. Similarly, phase-in treatment applies to self-constructed business property of an entity (or direct owner), where construction of the property to be used in the activity commenced on or before August 16, 1986.

When you own both pre-October 23, 1986, and post-October 22, 1986, interests in passive activities, this order is followed in calculating the phase-in. Determine the amount that would be disallowed absent the phase-in. Phase-in relief then applies to the lower of the total passive loss, or the passive loss taking into account only pre-October 23, 1986 interests.

EXAMPLE—

You have $100 of passive loss relating to pre-October 23, 1986, interests and $60 of net passive income from post-October 22, 1986, interests, resulting in a total passive loss of $40. The phase-in treatment applies to the lesser of $100 or $40.

Any passive loss that is disallowed for a taxable year during the phase-in period and carried forward is allowable in a later year only to the extent that there is net passive income in the subsequent year (or there is a fully taxable disposition of the activity).

EXAMPLE—

You have a passive loss of $100 in 1987, $65 of which is allowed; under the phase-in, $35 is carried forward. The $35 is not allowed in a later year under the phase-in percentage applying for that year. If you have a passive loss of $35 in 1988, including the amount carried over from 1987, then no relief under the phase-in is provided. If you have a passive loss of $50 in 1988 ($35 from 1987 and $15 from 1988, all attributable to pre-October 23, 1986, interests) then $6 of losses (40 percent of the $15 loss arising in 1988) is allowed against active income under the phase-in rule. The $35 loss carryover from 1987 is disallowed in 1988 and is carried forward (along with the disallowed $9 from 1988) and allowed in any later year in which you have net passive income.

The phase-in percentage applies to the passive loss net of any part of the loss that may be allowed under the $25,000 allowance rule for rental activity.

SUSPENDED LOSSES ALLOWED ON DISPOSITION OF YOUR INTEREST

Suspended losses are allowed when you sell the passive income property in a taxable exchange. They are not allowed in tax-free exchanges and in sham transactions involving a repurchase option. A sale to a related party may not be treated as a disposition.

Worthlessness of a security in a passive activity may be treated as a disposition.

A disposition of your entire interest in a limited partnership will allow you to claim suspended deductions from the activity. However, the fact that the nature of an activity changes in the course of its development is not a disposition.

When the passive interest is given away, the donee's basis in the property may be increased by the suspended loss if the property is sold at a gain.

On the death of an investor in a passive interest, suspended losses are deductible on the decedent's final return to the extent gains would have been realized on a sale of the interest.

EXAMPLE—

Brown dies owning a limited partnership interest in a building. The basis of the interest is $30,000; its fair market value is $60,000. Suspended losses amount to $45,000. On Brown's final return, $15,000 of the loss may be deducted, that is, the amount of the suspended loss of $45,000 less gain of $30,000. If the suspended loss was $30,000 or less, there would be no deduction.

PORTFOLIO INCOME OF A PASSIVE ACTIVITY IS NOT PASSIVE INCOME

Portfolio income such as interest, dividend, royalty, or annuity income earned on funds set aside for future use in the activity is not treated as passive income from the activity and must be accounted for separately. Gain or loss from sales or exchanges of portfolio assets (including property held for investment) is treated as portfolio gain or loss. Portfolio income is reduced by the deductible expenses (other than interest) that are directly allocable to such income. Properly allocable interest expense also reduces portfolio income. Thus, such deductions are not treated as attributable to a passive activity.

Allocation of interest to portfolio income may be made on the basis of assets or traced to a particular transaction.

In the case of closely held corporations, the passive loss rule permits passive losses (and credits, in a deduction equivalent sense) to offset net active income, but not portfolio income. For example, if a closely held corporation has $400,000 of passive losses from a rental activity, $500,000 of active business income, and $100,000 of portfolio income, the passive losses may be applied to reduce the active business income to $100,000, but not applied against the portfolio income.

TAX CREDITS OF PASSIVE ACTIVITIES LIMITED

You may not claim a tax credit from a passive activity unless you report and pay taxes on income from a passive activity. Further, the tax allocated to that income must be at least as much as the credit. If the tax credit exceeds your tax liability on income allocable to passive activities, the excess credit is not allowed.

EXAMPLE—

You have a $1,000 credit from a passive activity. You do not report income from any passive activity. You may not deduct the credit because no part of your tax is attributed to passive activity income. The credit is suspended until you have income from a passive activity and tax on the income is incurred. All or part of the credit may then be claimed to offset the tax. If you dispose of your interest, before using a suspended credit, the credit may no longer be claimed.

Real estate allowance.   Where the credit is from rental real estate, a *deduction equivalent* of up to $25,000 may allow a credit that otherwise would be disallowed. You must meet the active participation tests in the year the credit arose. The $25,000 allowance is subject to the regular phase-out rule. In the case of the low-income housing and rehabilitation credit, however, you need not meet the active participant test and the phase-out for the $25,000 allowance starts at AGI of $200,000 and the deduction equivalent is completely disallowed when AGI reaches $250,000. In the case of the low-income housing credit, the increase in the phase-out range and waiver of the active participation rule apply only to property placed in service before 1990, and during the original credit compliance period for the property, except if the property is placed in service before 1991 and 10 percent or more of the total project costs are incurred before 1989.

The *deduction equivalent* of a credit is the amount which, if allowed as a deduction, would reduce your tax by an amount equal to the credit. For example, a tax credit of $1,000 in the 35 percent bracket is equal to a deduction of $2,857 and would come within the $25,000 allowance provided you actively participated. In the 35 percent bracket the equivalent of a $25,000 deduction is a tax credit of $8,750 ($25,000 x 35%). In the 28 percent bracket, it is $7,000. Thus, if you have a rehabilitation credit of $8,000 and you are in the 28 percent bracket, the $25,000 allowance may allow you to claim $7,000 of the credit, while $1,000 of the credit would be held in suspense.

Basis adjustment for suspended credits.   If the basis of property was reduced when tax credits were claimed, you may elect to add back a suspended credit to basis when the property is disposed.

EXAMPLE—

Jones places in service rehabilitation credit property and claims an allowable credit of $50, which also reduces basis by $50. However, under the passive loss rule, he is prevented from claiming the credit. In a later year, he disposes of his entire interest in the activity, including the property whose basis was reduced. He may elect to increase basis of the credit property by the amount of the original basis adjustment.

If the property is disposed of in a transaction that, under the passive loss rule, is not treated as a fully taxable disposition, then no basis adjustment is allowed.

WORKING OIL AND GAS INTERESTS
OUTSIDE OF PASSIVE LOSS RESTRICTIONS

The passive loss rule does not apply to an investor who holds a working interest in an oil and gas property. This is true even if he does not materially participate in the activity.

A working interest is one burdened with the cost of developing and operating the property such as a share in tort liability (for example, uninsured losses from a fire); some responsibility to share in additional costs; responsibility for authorizing expenses; receiving periodic reports about drilling, completion and expected production; the possession of voting rights and rights to continue operations if the present operator steps out.

If your liability is limited, you are not treated as owning a working interest. For example, you are a limited partner or a stockholder in an S corporation.

Rights to overriding royalties or production payments, and contract rights to extract or share in oil and gas profits without liability for a share of production costs are not working interests.

INTEREST EXPENSES
AND OTHER DEDUCTIONS
OF PASSIVE ACTIVITIES

Interest deductions attributable to passive activities are subject to the passive loss rule but not to the investment interest limitations. For example, in 1987, if you have net passive loss of $100, $40 of which is of interest expense, the entire $100 is subject to limitation under the passive loss rule. No portion of the loss is subject to limitation under the investment interest limitation. Similarly, income and loss from passive activities generally are not treated as investment income or loss in calculating the amount of the investment interest limitation.

The passive loss rule applies to all deductions that are from passive activities, including deductions for state and local property taxes incurred with respect to passive activities whether or not such deductions are claimed above-the-line or as itemized deductions.

EXAMPLES—

1. In 1985, you invested as a limited partner in a syndicate holding rental property. In 1986, your share of the syndicate's loss is $5,000. Your other income is $100,000 made up of salary interest and dividend income. You may deduct the loss from your other income.

2. Assume in 1987, the loss from the syndicate is $6,000. You may deduct 65 percent of the loss or $3,900 under the phase-out from your other income.

3. Assume you invested in the syndicate in November 1986. In 1987 you may deduct no part of the loss because you made the investment after October 22, 1986. Further, you do not qualify for the $25,000 allowance because as a limited partner you do not meet the active participant test.

AT-RISK LOSS LIMITS APPLY TO REAL ESTATE

At one time, it was possible to claim loss deductions from an investment although the losses exceeded your actual investment or personal liability in the venture. The at-risk rules bar loss deductions once they exceed your cash or at-risk investment.

EXAMPLE—

You invest cash of $1,000 in a venture and sign a nonrecourse note for $8,000. Your share of the venture's loss is $1,200. The at-risk rules limit your deduction to $1,000, the amount of your cash investment; as you are not personally liable on the note, the amount of the liability is not included as part of your basis for loss purposes.

Under pre-1987 law, the at-risk rules applied to all investments except real estate ventures. Under the new laws the at-risk rules apply to real estate investments. However, many real estate ventures will escape the at-risk limits as the rules do not apply to nonrecourse financing from commercial lenders. Third party nonrecourse debt from a related lender, other than the seller, may also escape at-risk rules providing the terms of the loan are commercially reasonable and on substantially the same terms as loans involving unrelated persons. Thus, the at-risk rules will generally apply only to real estate ventures involving seller-financed arrangements.

The at-risk rules apply to real property placed in service after December 31, 1986, and for losses attributable to an interest in a partnership or S corporation or other pass-through entity acquired after December 31, 1986.

TRAVEL, ENTERTAINMENT, AND OTHER JOB EXPENSES

DEDUCTING TRAVEL, ENTERTAINMENT, AND MOVING EXPENSES

You may deduct expenses that are necessary to earn your salary. Typical expenses are those incurred for traveling to see customers or clients, food and lodging on business trips away from home, entertaining business customers, work clothes, and union and business association dues.

Job expenses are deducted on different schedules. One class of expenses is deductible from income before you itemize; others are deductible only if you claim itemized deductions. This difference in treatment is fixed by law. To understand the changes made by the new law first review how the pre-1987 law treats expenses on your 1986 return due April 15, 1987, and then the changes.

1986 job expenses deductible from gross income on Form 1040 whether or not you itemize deductions are:

Travel expenses away from home
Transportation expenses
Reimbursed expenses
Moving expenses

On your 1986 Form 1040, these deductions are claimed in the section titled "Adjustments to Income." Travel expenses away from home, transportation expenses, and expenses reimbursed by your employer are referred to as "employee business expenses." They may also be described as "above the line" deductions since they may be claimed even if you do not itemize.

Job expenses deductible in 1986 as itemized deductions (below the line) only if you claim excess itemized deductions are:

Unreimbursed entertainment expenses
Unreimbursed business gifts
Union dues
Uniform and work clothes costs

Exception for outside salespersons. The above "below the line" expenses are deductible from gross income if you are an outside salesperson.

Travel expenses incurred to look after investments are deducted as itemized deductions. Travel costs incurred to look after rental or royalty-producing property are deducted in Schedule E.

Starting in 1987, *unreimbursed* travel and transportation and moving expenses to a new job location are no longer deductible by employees above-the-line from gross income.

Unreimbursed travel and transportation expenses are deductible only as miscellaneous deductions and when added to other miscellaneous deductions are subject to the two percent AGI floor. Unreimbursed moving expenses are deductible only if you itemize deductions. However, moving expenses are not subject to the two percent AGI floor.

You may deduct the cost of moving to a new place of work or doing business if:

(1) The distance between your new place of work and your old home exceeds by at least 35 miles the distance between the former place of work and your old home; and

(2) You have been or will be working at the new location for at least 39 weeks as a full-time employee, or 78 weeks on a full-time self-employed basis.

The move should take place within one year from the time you first start to work at the new location. If not, the deduction for moving costs may be disallowed. However, the IRS may allow a deduction if you delayed your family's move so that your children could finish a school year.

TWO PERCENT FLOOR WILL REDUCE
MISCELLANEOUS DEDUCTIONS

Starting in 1987, a two percent floor applies to the total of most miscellaneous nonbusiness deductions. The purpose of the floor is to reduce or eliminate such deductions. The floor applies to the following deductions:

Unreimbursed travel, meals, and entertainment expenses
Union dues
Professional association dues
Work clothes expenses
Costs of looking for a new job, agency fees
Tax advice and preparation fees
Appraisal fees related to casualty losses and charitable property contributions, and
Investment expenses such as safe deposit rentals and fees to investment counselors
Deductible home office expenses
Deductible legal fees

The two percent floor does not apply to these miscellaneous expenses:

Gambling losses up to gambling income
Estate tax attributable to income in respect of a decedent
The deduction for repayment of amounts held under a claim of right
Impairment-related work expenses for handicapped employees
Amortizable bond premium
Certain costs of cooperative housing corporations
Interest expenses of short-sales
Certain terminated annuity payments

The following tables show the effect of the 2 percent floor on deductible expenses.

HOW TWO PERCENT FLOOR REDUCES DEDUCTION

If adjusted gross income is	And nonbusiness and investment expenses are							
	$200	$400	$600	$800	$1,000	$1,500	$2,000	$3,000
	You may deduct							
$ 5,000	100	300	500	700	900	1,400	1,900	2,900
10,000	0	200	400	600	800	1,300	1,800	2,800
15,000	0	100	300	500	700	1,200	1,700	2,700
20,000	0	0	200	400	600	1,100	1,600	2,600
25,000	0	0	100	300	500	1,000	1,500	2,500
30,000	0	0	0	200	400	900	1,400	2,400
35,000	0	0	0	100	300	800	1,300	2,300
40,000	0	0	0	0	200	700	1,200	2,200
50,000	0	0	0	0	0	500	1,000	2,000
60,000	0	0	0	0	0	300	800	1,800
70,000	0	0	0	0	0	100	600	1,600
80,000	0	0	0	0	0	0	400	1,400
90,000	0	0	0	0	0	0	200	1,200
100,000	0	0	0	0	0	0	0	1,000
150,000	0	0	0	0	0	0	0	0

If your AGI is	Nonbusiness miscellaneous expenses must exceed this amount for a deduction
$ 2,000	$ 40
5,000	100
10,000	200
15,000	300
20,000	400
25,000	500
30,000	600
35,000	700
40,000	800
50,000	1,000
60,000	1,200
70,000	1,400
90,000	1,800
100,000	2,000
200,000	4,000

In a conference report, Congress instructed the Treasury to write regulations applying the two percent floor to indirect deductions of pass-through entities (including mutual funds) other than estates, non-grantor trusts, cooperatives, and REITs. Thus, the two percent floor applies to grantor trusts, partnerships, and S corporations. In the case of an estate or trust, the adjusted gross income is computed like that of an individual, except that the deductions for administrative costs that would not have been incurred if the property were not held in such trust or estate are not subject to the floor.

IMPORTANCE OF REIMBURSEMENT ARRANGEMENTS

If your job requires you to incur deductible travel and entertainment expenses, sound tax planning requires that you and your company fix a definite policy of how the expenses will be borne. The best arrangement is for your company to give you an allowance or to reimburse you for the expenses. Try to avoid an understanding that your salary has been set to cover your payment of expenses. The following example illustrates the advantage of having a reimbursement arrangement which allows you to deduct from gross income expenses usually treated as itemized deductions.

Assume that it is understood between you and your company that your job requires paying entertainment expenses of $2,000 annually and that your net salary should be $38,000. If you are paid a straight salary of $40,000, which has to cover your payment of entertainment costs, you report $40,000 as salary income and you may deduct the $2,000 only if you itemize deductions. Further, your deduction is subject to a two percent adjusted gross income floor starting in 1987. If two percent of your adjusted gross income exceeds your unreimbursed entertainment expense, your payout is not deductible. Here, assuming $40,000 is also the amount of your adjusted gross income, $800 of your unreimbursed expense is not deductible. But if your salary is set at $38,000 and your company pays you for the entertainment costs, you report a salary of $38,000 plus $2,000 for entertainment less the $2,000 for actual entertainment costs. The amount reported on the return without the reimbursement arrangement is $40,000; with the reimbursement arrangement, it is $38,000.

If you are entitled to reimbursement from your employer, make sure you receive it. Failure to be reimbursed may prevent you from deducting your out-of-pocket expenses. A supervisor whose responsibility was to maintain good relations with his district and store managers entertained them and their families and also distributed gifts among them. His cost was $2,500 for which he could have been reimbursed by his company, but he made no claim. Consequently, the court disallowed it as a deduction on his return. The expense was the company's; any goodwill he created benefited it. But because he failed to seek reimbursement, he was not allowed to convert company expenses into his own.

PERFORMING ARTISTS GET SMALL TAX BREAK

A tax concession has been provided for performing artists with low incomes. They can deduct expenses as ''above-the-line'' deductions. This allows them to claim such deductions and also claim the standard deduction.

A performing artist may report acting income and expenses as independent contractors if he or she has:

(1) Two or more employers in the performing professions during the tax year with at least $200 of earnings from each;

(2) Expenses from acting or other services in the performing arts that exceed 10 percent of gross income from such work; and

(3) Adjusted gross income (before deducting these expenses) does not exceed $16,000.

Independent contractor status will allow a deduction of the expenses before claiming itemized deductions or the standard deduction.

If a performing artist is married, a joint return must be filed to claim the deduction, unless the couple live apart the whole year. If each spouse is a performing artist, the $16,000 adjusted income test applies to the couple's combined income, but each spouse must separately meet the two-employer test and 10 percent expense test to claim the "above-the-line" deduction.

QUIET BUSINESS MEAL RULE REPEALED AND NEW 80 PERCENT COST LIMITATION

Under pre-1987 law, the cost of dining was generally deductible if the meal took place in an atmosphere conducive to business discussions. That business was not actually discussed before, during, or after the meal did not jeopardize the deduction. Further, you did not have to show that the meal expenses were either directly related to or associated with the active conduct of a trade or business. Under the new law, this "quiet business meal rule" no longer applies. Further, only 80 percent of allowable meal costs are deductible.

EXAMPLE—

During 1987, business meal costs of $2,000 are incurred. Only 80 percent of the costs are considered deductible. This amount is $1,600 ($2,000 × 80%). Further, if you are an employee and the costs are not reimbursed, the $1,600 plus miscellaneous deductions are subject to the two percent AGI floor.

With the repeal of the quiet meal rule, meal costs must meet the tests that have been and are currently applied to other types of entertainment expenses. That is, in addition to having to show that a meal or entertainment expense is ordinary and necessary to your business, the expense must also be: (1) directly related to the active conduct of your business, and (2) a business discussion must occur directly before, during, or following the entertainment activity. Further, you may not deduct lavish or extravagant meal costs and either you or your employee must be present during the meal. You may not deduct costs of a meal of business customers if neither you nor an employee attends the meal. This is true even if the parties discuss business related to your interest. However, the cost of the meal may be deductible as a business gift subject to a $25 annual limit per person. An independent contractor such as an attorney representing you may be treated as an employee.

According to a committee report, you do not have to meet the discussion rule when you travel away from home on business and eat alone or with your family or other personal acquaintances, and you claim a deduction only for your meal costs.

In 1987 and 1988, a full deduction is allowed for meal costs (if not separately stated) that are provided as an integral part of a meeting at a convention, seminar, annual meeting, or business meeting (including meetings held at an employee training facility) if:

(1) The program includes the meal;
(2) More that 50 percent of the participants are away from home;
(3) There are at least 40 attendees; and
(4) A speaker is present.

You may not deduct meal costs incurred in a meeting to discuss investment or tax planning with an investment or tax advisor.

ENTERTAINMENT EXPENSES ALSO SUBJECT TO 80 PERCENT COST RULE

Starting in 1987, only 80 percent of allowable entertainment expenses, such as country club dues and tickets, are deductible. If your employer reimburses your expenses, your employer, not you, is subject to the 20 percent reduction.

EXAMPLE—

In 1987, you incur reimbursed meal and entertainment costs of $5,000. Your employer, after reimbursing you, may claim a deduction of only $4,000 ($5,000 × 80%).

Theater or sporting event ticket costs.   Assuming that tickets have been bought for a valid business purpose, the deductible amount is 80 percent of the face value of the ticket including any tax. Under this rule, you may not deduct the additional amount paid a scalper or a ticket agency. For example you pay an agency $40 for a $30 ticket. You may deduct $24 (80% of $30).

Tickets bought for charitable fund raising sport events are not subject to the 80 percent and the face value rules if:

(1) The primary purpose of the event is to benefit a tax-exempt charitable organization, such as a church or school;
(2) The entire net proceeds go to that charity;
(3) Volunteers do substantially all the work performed in carrying out the event.

The entire cost of a ticket includes seating, parking and meals, which are fully deductible.

The cost of charity golf outings meets these tests according to a Congressional report even though prizes are offered to participating golfers and security personnel are hired. The fund raising exception does not cover high school or college games.

Skybox rental costs.   Companies generally rent skybox seats for the season. Between 1987 and 1989, deductions for the extra cost of skybox rentals will be phased out. Starting in 1989, deductions for rentals at more than one event may not exceed the sum of the face values of non-luxury box seat tickets for the number of seats in the box. The allowable amount is also subject to the 80 percent cost rule. In 1987 and 1988, there is a partial loss of deductions. In 1987, only one-third of the otherwise disallowed amount is disallowed; in 1988, two-thirds is disallowed.

A skybox is a facility at a sports arena that is separated from other seating and is available at a higher price than the price applicable to other seating. Separately stated charges for food or beverage charges at the box are deductible as entertainment expenses and are also subject to the 80 percent cost rule.

Other exceptions to 80 percent rule.   Not subject to the 20 percent reduction are traditional employer-paid recreational expenses for employees (the costs of a holiday party), items fully taxable as compensation or excludable from income as *de minimis* fringe benefits, and items sold to or made available to the general public (as promotional activities).

TRAVEL EXPENSES OF ATTENDING INVESTMENT CONVENTIONS AND SEMINARS

Under pre-1987 law, the costs of attending a business convention or seminar are deductible. Courts have also allowed deductions for the costs of attending investment conventions and seminars. Under the new law, no deduction is allowed for travel or other costs of attending an investment convention, seminar, or similar meeting. This disallowance rule does not apply to business conventions, seminars or sales meetings. However, according to a committee report, no deduction should be allowed for travel and other costs of attending a business convention or seminar where you merely receive a video tape of lectures on business topics to be viewed at your convenience and no other business-related activities or lectures occur during the convention.

RESTRICTIONS ON
CRUISE AND CHARITABLE AND
EDUCATIONAL TRAVEL COSTS

Under pre-1987 law, there were no special limits on deducting (1) business cruise costs, (2) educational travel costs, and (3) traveling expenses on trips sponsored by or for a charitable organization.

Under the new law, the following limits apply to such travel:

Luxury-water transportation.   Deductible cruise costs are limited to twice the highest federal *per diem* for travel in the United States times the number of days in transit.

EXAMPLE—

You sail to Europe on business. Assume that the highest *per diem* federal rate is $100 and the trip lasts four days. The deduction for the cost of the trip is $800 ($100 $\times$ 2 $\times$ 4).

The double *per diem* rule applies without regard to the 80 percent limit on meal costs if meals are not separately stated.

The above limitation does not apply to cruise ship convention costs that are deductible up to $2,000 a year, if all the ports of call are in the U.S. or U.S. possessions and if the ship is registered in the United States.

Educational travel.   No deduction is allowed for costs of travel claimed as a form of education. For example, no deduction will be allowed to a French teacher traveling to France to maintain general familiarity with the French language and culture or to a social studies teacher traveling to learn about or photograph people and customs.

The new law overrules Treasury regulations that allow deductions for travel as a form of education.

However, deductions are still allowed for travel that qualifies as a business expense. For example, if a teacher must travel abroad to do research that cannot be done elsewhere, the travel costs are deductible because the non-travel research or course costs are deductible business expenses. An employee's unreimbursed travel costs away from home are deductible after 1986 only as an itemized deduction subject to two percent of the adjusted gross income floor. Meal expenses are subject to the 80 percent deduction limit.

Charitable travel.   No deduction is allowed for charitable travel expenses (whether paid directly by the individual or indirectly through a contribution to the organization) unless there is *no* significant element of personal pleasure, recreation, or vacation in the travel away from home. This provision is primarily directed against the tax deductions claimed for trips organized by educational groups as research studies in vacation and exotic areas.

HOME OFFICE EXPENSES
OF EMPLOYEES

The law severely limits employees from claiming deductions for home office expenses by setting conditions most employees cannot meet. The office must be exclusively used on a regular basis as your principal place of business or as a place in which patients, clients, or customers meet or deal with you in the normal course of your profession or business. As an employee, it is only in rare situations that your home office is your principal place of business or a place for meeting patients, clients, or customers. Both the Tax Court and an appeals court agree with the IRS that making and receiving telephone calls at a home office is not the equivalent of clients' visits. However, an appeals court has developed a pro-taxpayer exception where an employer does not provide adequate working space. It has allowed home office expense deductions to a violinist working for the Metropolitan opera upon proof that the Met did not provide space for practice and to a professor who did substantial work at home because his school did not provide adequate office space.

To avoid the above restrictions, a CPA rented home office space to his employer. Knowing that a home office deduction would be disallowed by the IRS under the "principal place of business" test, the CPA, who worked at home, devised a rental arrangement with his firm. His firm rented his home office and garage for $5,400. He reported the rental income and deducted home office costs as offsetting rental expenses. A majority of the tax court upheld the rental arrangement. There was a bona fide business reason for the rental. The CPA needed private office space away from the firm's premises, and the logical place for that office was his home.

Under the new law starting in 1987, no home office deductions are allowed for an employee-employer rental arrangement such as that of the CPA.

Income limits on home office expenses.   Under pre-1987 law, the IRS held that for purposes of limiting the deduction for business area expenses, gross income means gross receipts reduced by those business expenses that are not allocable to the use of the home area itself, such as salary paid to an assistant or office supplies. This rule barred a home office expense deduction if expenses such as salaries equalled or exceeded the gross business receipts. A court rejected the IRS position.

EXAMPLE—

Smith does a sideline business consulting from a home office. His gross income from consulting services is $1,900. He paid an office secretary salary of $500, office telephone expenses of $150, and office supply costs of $200.

In addition, he allocated 10 percent of his home costs to the business space, as follows:

	Total	10% allocation
Mortgage interest	$5,000	$ 500
Real estate taxes	2,000	200
Insurance	600	60
Utilities	900	90
Depreciation	3,200	320

According to the IRS, the allocable deduction for business use was computed as follows:

Gross income from consulting		$1,900
Less: Secretary's salary	500	
Business phones	150	
Office supplies	200	850
Income from office		$1,050
Less: Interest	500	
Taxes	200	700
Balance		$ 350
Less: Insurance	60	
Utilities	90	150
Balance		200
Less: Depreciation		200

According to the IRS, only $200 of the allocable depreciation of $320 was deductible. The balance of interest and taxes was deductible as itemized deductions. The Tax Court disagreed and held deductions could be claimed against the $1,900 of gross income, rather than the reduced figure of $1,050.

Under a new law starting in 1987, the IRS rule is approved. That is, allowable home office deductions are limited to net income from the business (gross income less deductions attributable to the business). If expenses are not deductible because of this net income limitation, the expenses are carried forward to the next year and treated as home office expenses subject to the net income limitation in the following year.

Home office expenses claimed by an employee are also subject to the two percent AGI floor.

IRA AND OTHER RETIREMENT PLANS

NEW IRA RULES

Starting in 1987, you may make IRA contributions of up to $2,000, provided you have wage, salary, or self-employment earnings. If your earned income is less than $2,000, the contribution limit is 100 percent of your pay (or earned income if self-employed).

An IRA contribution for years after 1986 is deductible, if you meet one of these tests:

(1) Your adjusted gross income (AGI) does not exceed $25,000 if single or $40,000 if married on a joint return or

(2) You are not an active participant in an employer-maintained retirement plan for any part of the plan year ending within your taxable year. If you are married and file a joint return, neither you nor your wife must be an active participant in such a plan.

When your AGI exceeds $25,000 or $40,000 and you are in a company retirement plan, your deduction is reduced over the next $10,000 of AGI. If you are single and your AGI is $35,000 or over, you may not claim a deduction. If you are married and filing jointly, you may not claim a deduction when your AGI is $50,000 or over. If you are a married person filing separately and you are a participant in a company retirement plan, you may not make a deductible IRA contribution if your AGI exceeds $10,000.

If your AGI is in the phaseout range, you may figure your reduced deduction as follows:

Step 1. Figure how much your AGI exceeds the $25,000 or $40,000 floor, whichever applies to you.

Step 2. Subtract Step 1 from $10,000.

Step 3. Multiply Step 2 by .20 if your contribution is $2,000; .225 if $2,250 for spousal account.

EXAMPLES (All examples assume company plan coverage.)—

1. You are single and your AGI is $26,000. Your deductible contribution is $1,800.
>   Step 1. $1,000 ($26,000 - $25,000).
>   Step 2. $9,000 ($10,000 - $1,000).
>   Step 3. $1,800 ($9,000 x .20).

2. You are married filing jointly and contribute $2,000. Your AGI is $42,000. Your deductible contribution is $1,600.
>   Step 1. $2,000 ($42,000 − $40,000).
>   Step 2. $8,000 ($10,000 − $2,000).
>   Step 3. $1,600 ($8,000 × .20).

3. Same facts as in Item 2, but your spouse also qualifies to make IRA contributions. His or her maximum deduction is also $1,600. On a joint return, the total deduction is $3,200.

If the deduction limit does not come to a multiple of $10, the amount is rounded to the next lowest $10. For example, if you figure a deduction limit of $1,806, the deduction limit is $1,800.

$200 IRA deduction floor.   A special rule gives a $200 deduction if your AGI falls within the last $1,000 of the phase out range. When your AGI is over $34,000 (single) or over $49,000 (married,joint), your reduced deduction would be less than $200. However, a $200 deduction may be claimed by a single person with an AGI of over $34,000 but under $35,000 and by a married person filing jointly with an AGI of over $49,000 but under $50,000.

EXAMPLE—

Your AGI is $34,400 and you are single.
>   Step 1: $9,400 ($34,400 − $25,000)
>   Step 2: $600 ($10,000 − $9,400)
>   Step 3: $120 ($600 × .20)

Although $120 is the deductible limit under the above computation, you may deduct $200.

For purposes of determining the IRA deduction limit, AGI is calculated without regard to any deductible IRA contributions made for the taxable year.

Are you a participant in an employer plan? An employer retirement plan means:

(1) A qualified pension, profit-sharing, or stock bonus plan;
(2) A qualified annuity plan;
(3) A simplified employee pension;
(4) A plan established for its employees by the United States, by a state or political subdivision, or by any agency or instrumentality of the United States or a state or political subdivision; or
(5) A tax-shelter annuity.

Active participant status is determined without regard to whether your rights under an employer-maintained retirement plan are vested. You are considered an active participant in a defined benefit (pension) plan if you are eligible to participate in the plan, even if you elect not to participate. An unfunded deferred compensation plan of a state or local government or a tax-exempt organization is not considered an employer plan. If you are self-employed and set up a Keogh plan, you are considered to be a member of an employer retirement plan.

Nondeductible contributions. If you are barred from making a deductible contribution under the above rules, you may make nondeductible IRA contributions of up to $2,000 (or $2,250, in the case of a spousal IRA). If you are allowed a partial IRA deduction, you may make a nondeductible contribution to the extent the maximum deduction limit ($2,000, $2,250 or $4,000) exceeds the deductible limit. Thus, if you are limited to a $1,800 deduction because of your income, you may make a $200 nondeductible contribution. The only advantage to making nondeductible contributions is that earnings on the account accumulate tax free until withdrawn.

You must designate a nondeductible contribution on your tax return. Designated nondeductible contributions may be made up to the due date of your tax return for the taxable year (without extensions).

You may file an amended return for a taxable year and change the designation of IRA contributions from deductible to nondeductible or visa versa.

It is important to make a designation. If you fail to do so, then all IRA contributions are presumed to have been deductible, and are taxable upon withdrawal from the IRA. You may rebut this presumption evidence that the contributions were nondeductible.

If you overstate the amount of designated nondeductible contributions made for any taxable year, you are subject to a $100 penalty for each such overstatement unless you can demonstrate that the overstatement was due to reasonable cause.

Although there may be an advantage to making nondeductible contributions which benefit from a tax-free buildup of income, this benefit may be blunted by the withdrawal rules.

Distributions and withdrawals.   All of your IRA accounts are treated as one contract. All distributions during a taxable year are treated as one distribution. If you withdraw an amount from an IRA during a taxable year and you previously made both deductible and nondeductible IRA contributions, part of your withdrawal will be tax free and part will be taxable. The nontaxable amount is based on the ratio of the nondeductible IRA contributions over the year-end balance of all of your IRA accounts plus the amount of the distribution (see example below). This withdrawal rule will penalize you if you make nondeductible contributions and later decide to make withdrawals from the "nondeductible account." You may not claim that you are withdrawing only your tax-free contributions, even if your withdrawal is less than your nondeductible contributions.

The payer of an IRA account such as a bank will report withdrawals from an IRA account to the IRS as if they are taxable. It is up to you to keep records that show otherwise and to indicate the nondeductible contributions on your tax return as required by IRS instructions.

EXAMPLES—

1. For 1987, you make a $2,000 IRA contribution, $1,500 of which is deductible. You made no prior IRA contributions. In 1988, you make a nondeductible $2,000 IRA contribution to another IRA account. In 1989, you make no IRA contributions and withdraw

$1,000 from the 1987 account. At the end of 1989, both IRAs total $4,000. The $1,000 withdrawn is treated as a partial return of nondeductible contributions of $500 and is not taxable. The 50 percent percentage is based on a fraction: $2,500/$5,000, that is, total nondeductible contributions of $2,500 over the total year-end account balance of $4,000 plus the $1,000 distribution.

2. In 1987, you contribute $2,000 to a nondeductible IRA; in 1988, another $2,000. In 1989, you may decide to withdraw $1,000 from that account. Assume you also have an IRA of $46,000 made up of deductible contributions and earnings on the contributions. At the end of 1989, both IRA accounts total $49,000. On the $1,000 withdrawal, only eight percent is attributed to your nondeductible investments. The eight percent figure is the percentage of your nondeductible contribution of $4,000 divided by $50,000, the $49,000 year-end balance plus $1,000 withdrawal. Thus $80 (8% of $1,000) is considered a nontaxable return of your money; $920 is taxable.

Therefore, if you have considerable IRA holdings especially from rollovers, there are tax traps in investing in a nondeductible account. If you withdraw amounts from your nondeductible account, you will incur tax. However, nondeductible contributions may be advisable, if you intend to keep money in the account for a buildup of funds until retirement.

LUMP-SUM AVERAGING RESTRICTIONS

The new law repeals 10-year averaging after 1986 for taxpayers who are under age 50 as of January 1, 1986. They may elect five-year averaging after they reach age 59½. This means that if a person who is under age 50 as of January 1, 1986, separates from service in 1987 or a later year, five-year averaging will not be allowed if he or she is under age 59½ when the distribution is made. Only one lifetime election is allowed. Under pre-1987 law, averaging was allowed to those under 59½ upon separation from service.

Those age 50 or older as of January 1, 1986, have one lifetime election after 1986 to use 10-year averaging based on 1986 rates or five-year averaging under rates effective in the year of distribution. They may make the election for a lump-sum distribution even if they are under 59½.

For 1986 distributions, capital gain treatment is still available for the portion of a lump sum attributable to pre-1974 contributions; an election may be made to report the entire distribution as ordinary income subject to 10-year averaging.

For distributions after 1986, capital gain treatment will be phased out between 1987 and 1991 for those who were under age 50 as of January 1, 1986. Under this phaseout rule, 100 percent of the pre-1974 portion of a 1987 distribution will qualify as capital gain if an election is made. In 1988, 95 percent of the pre-1974 portion will qualify, 75 percent in 1989, 50 percent in 1990, and 25 percent in 1991; after 1991 no part of the lump sum will qualify. Only one election may be made in 1987-1991 to apply these phase-out percentages. If the one-time election is made, five-year averaging for a later lump-sum distribution is barred.

Those age 50 or older as of January 1, 1986, will be allowed a one-time election to have the pre-1974 portion of a lump sum treated as capital gain, to be taxed at a 20 percent rate. This election will not be subject to the phaseout.

If you qualify for averaging, you must consider whether averaging will provide you with more retirement benefits after taxes than available through a rollover to an IRA. Also be aware that a lump-sum payment exceeding $562,500 may be subject to an excess retirement penalty.

Instead of paying tax now, you may defer tax by making a tax-free rollover; simply transfer your lump-sum distribution to an IRA or to a qualified plan of a new employer within 60 days of receipt. When payouts from IRAs are made, they are taxed at ordinary-income rates; you lose forever your right to averaging if you roll over your distribution to an IRA. You can not defer indefinitely the payment of income tax on the lump sum. You must begin to receive distributions after age 70½ or be subject to a penalty tax for insufficient withdrawals. Before making a tax-free rollover, figure your current tax on the lump-sum distribution. Compare it with an estimate of tax payable on a later disposition of the rolled over account.

Rules for making rollovers are as follows: If you receive one payment from your plan which includes all you are owed, the 60-day period starts with the date of that payment. If the distribution is in several payments, the 60-day period starts from the date of the last payment, provided all the payments are made within one taxable year. For example, you retire in July 1987 and receive a partial distribution from your company plan. You are told that you will receive the balance by December 1987. Provided all payments are received before the end of 1987, the payments received in July and December are considered a lump-sum distribution eligible for rollover. You have 60 days from the date of the final December payment to complete the rollover.

Your employer's retirement plan may invest in a limited amount of life insurance. The insurance contract may then be distributed to you as part of a lump-sum retirement distribution. Tax on a lump sum may generally be avoided through a rollover to an IRA or other qualified plan. However, you may not roll over a life insurance contract to an IRA. The law specifically bars investment of IRA funds in life insurance contracts. Thus if you receive a lump-sum distribution of cash and a life insurance contract, the cash (less your own contributions) may be rolled over tax free to an IRA. The insurance contract may be rolled over, and the value of the contract, less your contribution, is taxed in the year of distribution. However, if within 60 days of the distribution you take a position with another company which has a qualified plan that does not bar investments in life insurance contracts, you may make a tax-free rollover of the insurance contract to the new employer's plan.

A rollover does not allow you to avoid payment of tax. It merely postpones payment to some future date. The decision to make a rollover involves an evaluation of present and future needs, as well as the tax consequences of the rollover. If you need the funds immediately, perhaps to buy a retirement home or to start a business for your retirement years, you will not roll over the distribution. If you do qualify for averaging but do not have a pressing need for the funds, consider a rollover only after weighing the investment consequences of postponing tax through rollovers with the payment of immediate tax using averaging.

DEFINED-BENEFIT PLANS

Under prior law, defined-benefit plans were subject to a maximum benefit ceiling of $90,000 which had to be actuarially reduced for benefits beginning before age 62. However, for benefits payable before age 55, the reduction could not be below the actuarial equivalent of $75,000 annual benefit starting at age 55. The maximum $90,000 limit was also reduced under prior law by 10 percent ($9,000) for each year of service below ten years.

Under the new law, for plan years beginning after 1986, where an employee's benefit exceeds the maximum $90,000 limit, the $90,000 limit must be actuarially reduced for all benefits payable before the Social Security retirement age, currently 65. The reduced maximum benefit is the actuarial equivalent of a $90,000 annual benefit starting at age 65. The $75,000 floor for retirement at or after age 55 is repealed. If plan benefits begin after age 65 the $90,000 limit is increased so that it is the actuarial equivalent of a $90,000 benefit starting at age 65.

Under an important exception, the new benefit reduction rules will not adversely affect employees who in plan years before 1987 had already accrued benefits, which in terms of an annual benefit, exceeded the new limit allowed under the 1986 Act. To qualify for the exception, the plan had to be in existence on May 6, 1986, and accrued benefit had to be no more than the prior law benefit limit.

The $90,000 maximum benefit is also reduced for employees who have less than ten years of plan participation, as opposed to less than ten years of service as under prior law. The $90,000 limit is reduced by 10 percent per year for each year of participation below ten, but not below $9,000.

WHEN RETIREMENT BENEFITS
MUST BE RECEIVED

Generally, you must start to take benefits by April 1 of the calendar year following the year in which you reach age 70½ unless you continue working, in which case benefits must begin by April 1 following the year of retirement. However, if you are a five percent owner, you start to take benefits by April 1 following the year you reach 70½, whether or not you retire.

Distributions from an IRA must begin no later than April 1 of the calendar year following the year in which you reach 70½.

Payments must generally be over your life expectancy or the joint lives of yourself and a beneficiary. A 50 percent penalty applies if less than the minimum required IRA distribution is made. The penalty does not apply to insufficient distribution from plans other than IRAs.

New starting date after 1988.   A uniform starting date for benefits under all qualified plans, IRAs, and tax-sheltered annuities will generally take effect in 1989. Distributions after 1988 must commence no later than April 1 of the calendar year following the year in which you reach age 70½. You will no longer be able to defer the receipt of benefits from a qualified plan by continuing to work past age 70½.

Failure to satisfy the minimum distribution rules would trigger a nondeductible excise tax of 50 percent on the excess of the required minimum distribution over the actual distribution. The IRS may waive the penalty if the shortfall was due to reasonable error and steps are taken to remedy the shortfall.

An exception to the law protects employees who have attained age 70½ by January 1, 1988, provided they were not five percent owners at any time in the plan year ending in the calendar year in which they reach age 66½ or any subsequent plan year. Such individuals may continue to defer benefit payments until retirement.

There are also exceptions for employees who made a designation before 1984 of a retirement payout method qualifying under prior law.

Further, the effective date of the age 70½ distribution requirement is deferred for employees covered by a collective bargaining agreement ratified before March 1, 1986. The requirement will not apply to plan years starting before the *earlier* of:

(1) The date on which the collective bargaining agreement terminates (without considering extensions after February 28, 1986), but no later than January 1, 1989, or

(2) January 1, 1991.

WITHDRAWALS FROM QUALIFIED PLAN BEFORE ANNUITY STARTING DATE

Under prior law, distributions from a qualified plan before the annuity starting date were not taxable until you received all of your own contributions. A less favorable rule applies under the new law. Generally, for distributions after July 1, 1986, employee contributions are recovered pro rata. The tax-free portion of a pre-annuity distribution equals the ratio of your total contributions to your vested account balance as of the distribution date.

There are exceptions to the new rule. If withdrawals of employee contributions before separation from service were allowed under your plan as of May 5, 1986, the new pro rata rule applies only to the extent that pre-annuity distributions after 1986 exceed the investment in the contract as of December 31, 1986.

If employee contributions have been made to a defined contribution plan or a separate account of a defined tax benefit plan, withdrawals of employee contributions will be partly tax free and partly taxable. The part allocable to employee contributions is tax free, the part allocable to earnings in the contribution is taxed. If the account balance attributable to employee contributions loses value so that the total contributions cannot be recovered, the employee may deduct a loss.

PENALTY FOR EXCESS RETIREMENT DISTRIBUTIONS

Distributions after 1986 from an IRA or a qualified employer plan may be subject to a 15 percent penalty if they exceed specified ceilings. The penalty is in addition to regular tax. Penalty rules are complicated, and there are exceptions which may enable you, with careful planning of distributions, to avoid the penalty.

In general, you do not have to worry about the penalty if your total distributions for the year are $112,500 or less. The $112,500 ceiling applies to all qualified retirement distributions including IRA and annuity distributions.

A higher ceiling applies to lump-sum distributions for which special averaging may be claimed. No penalty applies to a lump sum unless it exceeds $562,500.

Exceptions. These are not subject to the excess retirement distribution plans penalty:

(1) Amounts attributable to your own contributions to an annuity contract or to a qualified employer plan;
(2) Distributions from a qualified plan rolled over to an IRA or other qualified plan;
(3) Distributions from your account ordered by a domestic relations court to be paid to a former spouse; the distribution is treated as that spouse's retirement distribution, not yours; and
(4) Distributions received by a beneficiary of a deceased individual.

Exception for pre-August 1, 1986, benefits. In addition to the exceptions discussed above, there are special rules that could eliminate or reduce any penalty for benefits that were accrued as of August 1, 1986. If such accrued benefits exceed $562,500, and you receive a distribution in 1987 or 1988, you may elect to treat the portion attributable to the pre-August 1, 1986, accruals as not subject to the penalty. If you do not make the election, a $150,000 exemption applies instead of the general $112,500 exemption.

EXAMPLE—

As of August 1, 1986, Jones has an $800,000 retirement account balance. In 1988, when his account is $900,000, he withdraws $600,000. He elects to treat a part of the distribution as attributable to pre-August 1, 1986, accruals. The percentage of accrual is 89 percent (800,000 divided by 900,000). Thus, 89 percent of the distributions or $534,000 is not subject to 15 percent excise tax.

Because of the complicated nature of these penalties, consult your plan administrator and Treasury regulations before taking a distribution exceeding the applicable $112,500 or $562,500 floor.

DEATH TAX PENALTY

The new law imposes a 15 percent estate tax if you die having an "excess retirement accumulation." This tax generally applies where the value of a decedent's interests in all qualified plans, annuities, and IRAs exceeds the present value of annual payments equal to the $112,500 ceiling over the deceased individual's life expectancy immediately before death. The Treasury is to release rules for making this computation, including the use of a reasonable interest rate in figuring present value.

The penalty applies to estates of persons dying after 1986 and is calculated separate and apart from any estate tax liability due on a decedent's other assets. Further estate tax credits may not offset the tax.

REPEAL OF THREE-YEAR COST RECOVERY RULE

Under prior law, if you received retirement benefits in the form of an employee annuity and you contributed to the policy, you were allowed to recover your cost before reporting income, if, within three years of the first payment, payments under the contract equaled or exceeded your cost.

EXAMPLE—

Starting July 1, 1985, Jones received a pension annuity of $300 a month for the rest of his life. He contributed $9,000 to the policy; his company paid the balance. Because payments would equal or exceed cost within three years, payments received before January 1, 1988, are not taxable income.

Payments in	Total
1985 (six months)	$1,800
1986	$3,600
1987	$3,600
	$9,000

Under the new law, the three-year recovery rule is repealed for annuities starting after July 1, 1986. Payments under post-July 1, 1986, annuities are reported according to regular annuity rules which consider your life expectancy and cost contributions. If you made no cost contributions, all of your payments are taxed. If you did contribute, part of your yearly payments are treated as income and part as a tax-free return of your cost contribution.

Your total tax-free exclusion cannot exceed your total contributions for annuities starting after 1986. Under prior law, individuals who lived longer than their projected life expectancy could exclude more than their contributions. If an annuitant dies before recovering all of his or her contributions, the unrecovered amount may be deducted on his or her final tax return.

TAX BENEFITS OF SALARY-DEFERRED PLANS (401(k)) ARE LIMITED

Under prior law, employees could defer up to the lower of 25 percent of pay or $30,000. The new law reduces the ceiling to $7,000, which will be indexed for cost-of-living increases. The annual $7,000 ceiling applies to total salary-reduction contributions to 401(k) plans and also to Simplified Employee Pensions (SEPs).

The new law also imposes stricter discrimination rules. Under prior law, the average of deferrals as a percent of compensation for the highest paid eligible employees (1/3) could not exceed 150 percent of the actual deferral percentage of the lowest paid two-thirds of eligible employees. Alternatively, the actual deferral percentage of the top one-third could not exceed the lesser of 250 percent of the actual deferral percentage of the lowest two-thirds of employees, or the actual deferral percentage of the lowest two-thirds of employees plus three percentage points.

Under the new law, the deferral percentage by an employer's highly compensated employees may not exceed 125 percent of the deferral percentage of eligible nonhighly compensated employees. Alternatively, the deferral percentage of an employer's highly compensated employees may not exceed 200 percent of the deferral percentage of the nonhighly compensated employees, or the actual deferral percentage of the nonhighly compensated employees plus two percentage points.

Further, the creation of a salary reduction plan will not help to qualify another company plan under the general coverage and non-discrimination tests. Thus a plan that does not meet the anti-discrimination rule may not be joined with a salary reduction plan to satisfy the rule. Finally, beginning in 1989, a salary reduction plan may exclude employees otherwise eligible to participate in a plan only if they have less than one year of service.

Tax on excess salary reduction contributions.   Amounts contributed over the $7,000 ceiling are taxed retroactively in the year of the salary reduction. Further, deferrals that are not distributed from the plan by the first April 15 after the close of the employer's tax year are treated as a pre-tax contribution and taxed again upon distribution. For example, in 1987, an employee defers $9,000. He must receive a distribution of the excess of $2,000 plus the income earned by April 15, 1988. The distribution is taxable to the employee in 1987 rather than 1988. If the excess is not distributed by April 15, 1988, it is taxable not only in 1987, but also on distribution from the plan.

The $7,000 limit applies to each employee. An employee who works for more than one firm should be aware that each plan does not entitle him to a separate $7,000 limit. If he is a member of more than one plan and contributions exceed $7,000 for all plans, he must receive a timely distribution of the excess or he will be subject to a double tax as explained above.

Ten percent excise tax.   The new law imposes a 10 percent excise tax on an employer for contributions of highly compensated employees that violate the nondiscrimination rules. To avoid the tax, the excess contributions must be distributed with income within two and a half months after the close of the plan year of the contribution. Excess contributions plus income distributed within the two and a half month period are treated as received by the employee in his taxable year in which the excess contributions would have been received. If the excess contributions plus income are distributed after the two and a half month period and before the close of the plan year, the amounts are reported by the employee in the year of distribution. Also, the plan may lose qualified status if distributions are not made by the end of the plan year after the plan year in which the excess contributions are made.

The new rules are generally effective in years beginning after December 31, 1986.

SIMPLIFIED EMPLOYEE PENSION PLANS (SEPS)

To avoid the administrative burdens of setting up a pension plan, an employer may set up a simplified employee pension plan, or SEP, and make IRA contributions on behalf of employees under much more favorable rules than apply to regular IRAs. For 1986, an employer could contribute up to the lesser of 15 percent of compensation or $30,000 to an employee's SEP. The employee must include the employer's contribution in income but may then claim an offsetting deduction.

After 1986, the new law allows employees in small companies to use salary reductions to make SEP contributions. The employee may direct the employer to contribute a portion of his salary to the SEP instead of receiving it in cash. If salary reductions are allowed under the following tests, the maximum salary reduction contribution by an employee is $7,000, the same limit as for elective deferrals under a 401(k) plan. The $7,000 limit may be increased starting in 1988 by an inflation factor. Salary reductions are allowed for a year only if the employer had more than 25 employees at any time during the prior taxable year. Further, at least 50 percent of the employees must elect the salary reduction option and the deferral percentage for highly compensated employees cannot be more than 125 percent of the average contribution by regular employees.

The maximum SEP contribution, including employer contributions and elective employee contributions, is still the lesser of 15 percent of pay or $30,000, with the $30,000 limit subject to inflation adjustments after 1987.

Employer contributions after 1986 to a SEP on behalf of an employee will be excluded from the employee's pay rather than included as under prior law, with the offsetting deduction.

If the employer contributes on behalf of any employee, the employer must contribute for all employees age 21 or over (earning at least $300) who have worked in at least three of the prior five years. If any employee is allowed to make elective SEP contributions under a salary reduction arrangement, all employees meeting the age and service test must be eligible to make elective contributions.

LOANS FROM QUALIFIED PLANS

Employees may borrow from a company plan without incurring tax if the loan is within certain limits and is paid back within a specified period. If the present value of an employee's vested accrued benefit is $20,000 or less, an employee is not taxed if the loan, when added to other outstanding loans from the plan, is $10,000 or less. This rule has not been changed by the new law. If your vested benefit exceeds $20,000, a loan in 1986 is not taxed if, when added to outstanding loans, it does not exceed the lesser of $50,000 or 50 percent of the vested benefit; loans after 1986 are subject to a reduced limit discussed below.

The repayment period under prior law was five years for all loans other than loans used to acquire, construct, or improve a principal residence for the employee or for a child or other family member.

The new law reduces (1) the $50,000 loan limit if there are other outstanding loans, (2) makes changes to the repayment provisions, and (3) imposes new interest deduction restrictions. The new rules apply to loans made after 1986. A renegotiation, renewal, or loan extension after 1986 of a pre-1987 loan is also considered a new loan subject to the new law.

Loan limits.   After 1986, a loan, when added to other outstanding loans, may not exceed $50,000 less the difference between (1) the highest outstanding loan balance during the one-year period ending the day before the loan and (2) the balance on the day of the new loan.

EXAMPLE—

Your vested plan benefit is $200,000. In January 1987 you borrow $30,000 from the plan. On November 1, 1987, when the outstanding balance on the first loan is $20,000, you want to take another loan without incurring tax. You may borrow an additional $20,000 without incurring tax. The $50,000 limit is first reduced by the outstanding loan balance of $20,000, leaving $30,000. The reduced $30,000 limit is in turn reduced by $10,000, the excess of $30,000 (the highest loan balance within one year of the new loan) over $20,000 (the balance on November 1).

Under prior law, you would have been able to borrow an additional $30,000 without incurring tax: $50,000 limit less $20,000 outstanding loan.

Repayment.   Loans after 1986 to buy a principal residence for yourself are still exempt from the five-year repayment requirement. However, loans to build or improve your principal residence will have to be repaid within five years. Further, the five-year repayment rule applies after 1986 on loans to finance the purchase of a home or home improvements for other family members.

Loans after 1986 must generally be repaid according to a level amortization schedule over the loan term with payments made at least quarterly. An employee may accelerate repayment, and the employer may require full repayment if you leave the company.

Interest deductions on loans.   Under prior law, deductions were allowed for interest on loans from a qualified plan. Under the new law, interest deductions on plan loans used for personal purposes will only be partially deductible from 1987 to 1990 under the five-year phaseout for consumer interest and nondeductible after 1990. Loans used for investment purposes will be subject to the new limits on investment interest. Further, key employees (generally owners and officers) are not allowed to claim interest deductions on plan loans made after 1986. Finally, if an employee borrows his own elective deferrals to a 401(k) plan or a tax-sheltered annuity plan, no interest deduction for the loan may be claimed for loans made after 1986.

TAX-SHELTERED ANNUITIES

Tax-exempt educational, religious, or educational organizations can set up annuity plans which allow employees to finance the purchase of an annuity contract through a salary reduction. The law does not tax the salary reduction if it is within a specified limit. Generally, the contribution is tax-free if it does not exceed (1) 20 percent of compensation multiplied by the number of years of service, less (2) tax-free contributions made in prior years to all employer qualified plans.

Under the new law, an additional limit is imposed. Elective contributions made through a salary reduction agreement may not exceed $9,500. This is higher than the $7,000 deferral limit under 401(k) and SEP plans. Starting in 1988, the $7,000 401(k) limit can be increased by the inflation adjustment. When the $7,000 limit is increased above $9,500, the $9,500 limit for tax-sheltered annuities will also be increased.

If an employee makes salary reduction contributions to a tax-sheltered annuity and also to a 401(k) plan or a SEP, the overall limit for the total salary reductions on all such plans is generally $7,000 but this is increased up to $9,500 for tax-sheltered annuity salary reductions.

The $7,000 and $9,500 limits apply only to elective contributions under salary reduction arrangements and not to employer contributions. Total employee plus employer contributions cannot exceed the contribution limit for defined contribution plans, which is the lower of 25 percent of pay or $30,000.

Special deferral limit for 15-year employees. Employees of qualified organizations who have completed at least 15 years of service are allowed to make higher salary reduction contributions after 1986 under a special rule. Employees of educational organizations, churches, hospitals, and health and welfare agencies qualify. Computation of the extra contribution is complicated. Generally, the additional contributions may not exceed $3,000.

Because of the complexity of these special contribution rules, we suggest you consult with your plan administrator for further details.

WITHDRAWALS BEFORE AGE 59½ FROM IRA's and QUALIFIED PLANS

Under prior law, a 10 percent penalty was imposed on IRA withdrawals before age 59½, unless made because of death or disability. A similar penalty applied to early withdrawals from qualified plans by five percent owners.

Under the new law, after 1986, the 10 percent penalty applies to premature withdrawals from all qualified corporate and Keogh plans and tax-sheltered annuity plans as well as IRAs. Distributions after 1986 that are made before age 59½, disability, or death are potentially subject to the penalty. However, there are exceptions. The penalty does not apply to IRA distributions that are part of a scheduled series of level payments under an annuity for the life of the participant or the joint lives of the owner and the owner's beneficiary. The same exception applies to qualified plan distributions starting after separation from service.

Further, the following exceptions to the penalty will be allowed for distribution from qualified plans:

(1) Withdrawals upon early retirement after age 55;
(2) Withdrawals used to pay deductible medical expenses exceeding 7.5 percent of adjusted gross income

(whether or not an itemized deduction for medical expenses is claimed);

(3) Withdrawals paid to an alternate payee pursuant to a qualified domestic relations court order;

(4) A lump-sum distribution before March 16, 1987, if you separated from service in 1986 and you pay 1986 tax on the distributions;

(5) Distributions made pursuant to a designation under the 1982 Tax Act (TEFRA); and

(6) Distributions to an employee who separated from service by March 1, 1986, provided that accrued benefits were in pay status as of that date under a written election specifying the payout schedule.

(7) Distributions before 1990 from an employee stock ownership plan (ESOP) provided that on average, a majority of the assets in the plan have been invested in employer securities for the five plan years before the plan year in which the distribution is made.

(8) Distributions of qualifying dividends from an employee stock ownership plan (ESOP).

CONTRIBUTIONS TO PENSION AND OTHER PLANS

Under prior law, deductible annual employer contributions are generally limited to the greater of the amount needed to satisfy the minimum funding requirements of the pension plan or 25 percent of the aggregate compensation of covered employees. This limit does not apply when an employee participates in both a defined and money-purchase pension plan of the same employer.

Under the new law, if an employee participates in both a defined benefit and money-purchase pension plan then the employer's deduction generally would be limited to the greater of (1) the amount needed to satisfy the minimum funding requirements of the defined benefit pension plan, or (2) 25 percent of the aggregate compensation of covered employees.

COST-OF-LIVING ADJUSTMENTS

Beginning in 1988, indexing will adjust the defined benefit plan dollar limit to reflect post-1986 cost-of-living increases. No adjustments will be made to the $30,000 defined contribution plan limit until the limit equals 25 percent of the defined benefit plan limit. Thereafter, the defined contribution plan limit will be increased so that it equals 25 percent of the defined benefit plan limit.

Employees may make additional contributions to a qualified cost-of-living account under a pension plan, to provide post-retirement cost-of-living increases.

BUSINESS TAXES

INCOME ACCELERATION
ON INSTALLMENT SALES

The Treasury has convinced Congress that the installment sale method defers too much tax for sellers of property. To cripple or defeat the tax deferment benefits of installment sales, the new law applies a complicated calculation that accelerates taxable income currently even though installment payments are not made. Taxable income is based on a percentage applied to an average of all debt held by the taxpayer. The rules primarily apply to dealers of personal and real property and to sales of rental or business or income-producing property if the sale price exceeds $150,000. The rules do not apply to sales of property you use for personal purposes or farm property. Further, sellers of property on a revolving credit plan are no longer permitted to use the installment method after 1986 even on sales made before 1987. Sellers using revolving credit plans who are denied installment reporting may report adjusted income over a four-year period.

Installment income based on a percentage of debt and payables.   Several calculations are necessary to determine income to be reported on the basis of debt held. You must determine "allocable installment indebtedness" (AII) for each taxable year and treat that amount as a payment in the taxable year on outstanding "applicable installment obligations" of *that* taxable year.

Members of an affiliated group are treated as a single taxpayer for purposes of making this calculation.

Allocable installment indebtedness (AII) is determined by—

(1) Dividing the face amount of installment obligations outstanding at the end of the year by the sum of (a) the face amount of *all* installment obligations, and (b) the adjusted basis of all other assets of the taxpayer;

(2) Multiplying the result in step 1 by the "average quarterly indebtedness;" and

(3) Subtracting any AII that is attributable to applicable install-ment obligations arising in prior years that are outstanding at the end of the taxable year.

The following is a simple example of the principle of calculating installment income.

EXAMPLE—

In 1987, a company sells property for $250 at a profit. Its total assets outside of the $250 installment note total $1,000. Total debt is $200 in the first quarter of 1987, $250 in the second quarter, $400 in the third quarter, and $350 in the last quarter. Thus, the average quarterly debt is $300 ($1,200 divided by 4) Allocable installment indebtedness (AII) is $60.

$$\frac{\text{Installment debt of } \$250}{\$250 \ + \ \$1,000 \text{ assets}} \times \$300 \text{ average quarterly debt}$$

$$\frac{\$250}{\$1,250} = \frac{1}{5} \text{ of } \$300 = \$60$$

Although no payments were made, $60 is taxable income in 1987.

NOTE: If further installment sales are made in 1988, the AII of $60, under step 3 above, reduces AII computed in 1988 if the debt was still outstanding.

"Applicable installment obligations" are installment obligations of (1) sales after February 28, 1986, of property held for sale to customers, and (2) installment obligations from sales after August 16, 1986, of real property used in your business or held for the production of rental income and the selling price of the property is over $150,000. However, the AII income rules do not apply until 1987 to such sales.

In a later taxable year, payments that do not exceed AII allocated to the obligation are not taxable; payments exceeding allocated AII are reported under usual installment method rules.

Average indebtedness for the year is on a quarterly basis. All debts outstanding at the end of each quarter are totaled including accounts payable and accrued expenses, bank loans, and mortgage debt. However, an annual basis calculation may be permitted to a seller who does not regularly sell property on installment basis or in the ordinary course of business.

Timeshare and lot exceptions.   If an election is made, the new rules do not apply to obligations of an individual dealer provided the obligation is not guaranteed or insured by any third person other than an individual. Further, the obligation must arise from the sale of a "timeshare" or of unimproved land, the development of which will not be done by the seller of the land or any affiliate of the seller. Under the election, the seller must pay interest on the deferral of tax liability attributed to the use of the installment method. The interest rate charged is 100 percent of the applicable federal rate that would apply to the installment obligation received in the sale without regard to a three-month lookback rule.

An exception from the AII rules may also apply to certain sales of manufacturers to dealers.

WHEN FISCAL YEAR PARTNERSHIPS, S CORPORATIONS, AND PERSONAL SERVICE CORPORATIONS MUST CHANGE TO A CALENDAR YEAR

Fiscal years have been used to spread the reporting of income for stockholders and partners over two years while the firm claims a deduction in the fiscal year.

EXAMPLE—

A doctor operates through a professional corporation that has a January 31 fiscal year. For the fiscal year ended January 31, 1986, the corporation reported income of $150,000. But before the end of 1985, the doctor received a monthly salary of $10,000 or $120,000. In January 1986, the corporation paid him the remaining $30,000 and claimed a deduction of $150,000 for the fiscal year. The doctor reported the $120,000 in 1985 and $30,000 in 1986.

To end this practice, the new law requires all partnerships, S corporations, and personal service corporations to change their fiscal tax years to the tax year of the partners and stockholders. As almost all individuals report on the calendar year, the law is an order to adopt calendar years. Under the law, a partnership must have the same tax year as that of partners owning a majority interest, unless a good business reason is established for having the fiscal year.

A partnership is not required to adopt the tax year of majority interest partners unless the partners having the same tax year have owned a majority interest for the preceding three tax years. If the majority owners do not have the same taxable year, the partnership must adopt the same tax year as its principal partners. If the principal partners do not have the same taxable year, and no majority of partners have the same taxable year, the partnership must adopt a calendar year.

All S corporations are required to follow the new rules regardless of the year the S election was made.

If a business purpose is shown for a fiscal year, the Treasury will allow the fiscal year. Deferral of income for three months or less no longer justifies a fiscal year. Companies that have already obtained the Treasury permission for a fiscal year do not have to get permission again because of the law unless that year was based on a deferral of income.

Under an election, excess income generated by changes in years may be reported ratably over the first four tax years by the partners and stockholders.

CASH METHOD MAY BE RESTRICTED TO SMALL BUSINESSES

Business income is reported on either the accrual or cash basis. If you have inventories, you must use the accrual basis in your business. The new law generally restricts the cash basis to self-employed persons, S corporations, professional service corporations (PC), and partnerships of individuals.

Cash basis.   You report income items in the taxable year in which they are received; you deduct all expenses in the taxable year in which they are paid. Income is also reported under the cash basis if it is "constructively" received. You have "constructively" received income when an amount is credited to your account, subject to your control, or set apart for you and may be drawn by you at any time. In general, you deduct expenses in the year of payment. Expenses paid by credit card are deducted in the year they are charged. Expenses paid through a "pay by phone" account with a bank are deducted in the year the bank sends the check. This date is reported by the bank on its monthly statement.

Advance payments.   You may not deduct advance rent payments covering charges of a later tax year. The IRS applies a similar rule to advance payments of insurance premiums; however, an appeals court has allowed an immediate deduction.

The cash basis has this advantage over other accounting methods: You may defer reporting income by postponing the receipt of income. For example, if 1987 is a high income year, you might extend the date of payment of some of your customers' bills until 1988. But make certain that you avoid the constructive receipt rule. You may also postpone the payment of presently-due expenses to a year in which the deduction gives you a greater tax saving.

Accrual basis.   You report income that has been earned whether or not received, unless a substantial contingency affects your right to collect the income. The treatment of expenses is subject to a more rigid set of rules. Generally, a deduction for expenses is claimed the year economic performance has occurred.

Starting in 1987, the cash basis method may not be used by a C (regular reporting) corporation, partnerships with any C corporation partners, tax shelters, and certain tax-exempt trusts with unrelated business taxable income. There are however, important exceptions for small businesses and professional corporations. The cash basis may be used by a business which is not considered a tax shelter if its average annual gross receipts (less returns and allowances) are $5 million or less for the preceding three tax years, (2) a professional service corporation in the health field, law, accounting, engineering, architecture, actuarial science, performing arts, or consulting fields, (3) farmers with gross receipts up to $1 million, and (4) timber operators. To use the cash basis, a PC must show that all of its stock is substantially owned (95 percent in value) by employees or former employees performing services in the field, or their estates.

A tax shelter is generally any enterprise (other than a C corporation) if at any time interests in such enterprise have been offered for sale in any offering required to be registered with any Federal or state agency having the authority to regulate the offering of securities for sale. Regular syndicates and farm syndicates may also be considered tax shelters. The $5 million gross receipts exception does not apply to tax shelters.

If a business has to change from the cash method to the accrual method, the change in the accounting method is treated as a change initiated by the taxpayer with the Treasury's consent.

Income arising from the change may be reported over a period not to exceed four years, beginning with the first tax year after 1986. In the case of certain hospitals, the income adjustment may be reported over a 10-year period. Rest or nursing homes, day care centers, medical school facilities, research laboratories, or ambulatory care facilities are not considered hospitals.

ACCRUING PERSONAL SERVICE INCOME

Starting in 1987, a new accrual rule applies to income due for services which (based on experience) will not be collected in that year. Part of the income may be deferred until the year of collection. However, if interest or a penalty is charged for a failure to make a timely payment, income is reported when the amount is billed. Further, if discounts for early payments are offered, the full amount of the bill must be accrued; the discount for early payment is treated as an adjustment to income in the year payment is made.

The amount of income to be deferred is based on a percentage that considers billing and uncollectibles over the past five most recent years. The percentage is found by dividing the uncollectible amounts by the total billings during the five-year period. That percentage applied to the total billings during the tax year may be deferred. For example, if $200,000 was billed during the five-year period and $20,000 was uncollectible, the percentage is 10 percent, and 10 percent of the current billings may be deferred. If you do not have a five-year experience, you use the period you were in business.

The new rule does not apply to banks and public utilities.

CAPITALIZING INVENTORY COSTS

Direct material and labor costs of producing inventory are included in the cost of inventory and as the inventory items are sold, the costs are deducted as cost of goods sold. Indirect expenses may also be allocated to inventory costs. If they are, the tax deduction claimed for such expenses is deferred until the inventory items are sold. If the expenses were deducted directly, the tax reduction value of the expense deduction would be accelerated resulting in a current cash flow. A new law is designed to reduce the opportunity of taking immediate deductions for items allocable to inventory. Small businesses are generally exempted from the new rules.

Under the new law, the following costs must be included as part of the cost of goods sold whenever inventory is valued at cost. (This can happen if inventory is valued at (1) cost or at (2) cost or market, whichever is lower and cost is used):

Purchasing costs, such as wages or salaries of employees responsible for purchasing

Costs of prepackaging, assembly, and processing goods

Storage costs, insurance premiums, and taxes related to a warehouse, and warehouse personnel wages

General and administrative costs and retirement benefit costs allocable to purchasing, production, and warehousing.

The new rules do not apply to a business with average annual gross receipts of $10 million or less for the last three years, long-term contracts, farmers, timber, and certain oil and gas drilling costs.

NEW LIFO METHOD
FOR SMALL BUSINESSES

Starting in 1987, businesses with average gross receipts of $5 million or less may elect a simplified dollar-value LIFO method.

The method replaces the single inventory pool method. However, businesses currently using the single pool method can continue that method. If a business wants to change to the new simple method, it can do so without IRS consent. However, a business that had not originally elected LIFO may need IRS consent for the new method. The inventory pools are based on government statistics. For further details, refer to IRS publications on the subject.

BAD DEBT RESERVE
METHOD REPEALED

The reserve method allows an accrual business to claim current deductions for part of current receivables that are expected to become uncollectible in the future. To end this favorable deduction rule, the new law repeals the bad debt reserve method of deducting bad debts for taxpayers other than financial institutions. Under the new law, a deduction for a bad debt is to be claimed only when a specific debt becomes partially or wholly worthless.

The required change from the reserve method to the specific chargeoff method is considered a change in accounting method initiated by the taxpayer with IRS consent. The balance in a bad debt reserve is to be reported as income ratably over a four-year period. The amount reported is generally the full balance without offsets for any anticipated amounts that will not be collected. For guaranteed bad debt reserves, the reserve balance is first reduced by the suspense account balance. The remaining balance is reported ratably over four years.

REVISION OF LONG-TERM CONTRACT ACCOUNTING RULES

Under prior law, one of two methods of accounting were allowed for long-term contracts:

(1) Percentage of completion method. Income reported is based on a percentage of the contract completed during each taxable year; costs are currently deductible.
(2) The completed contract method. Here the gross contract price is included in income and costs are deducted in the year the contract is completed.

Under the new law, the completed contract method is no longer available except under a small construction exception. If the exception does not apply, long-term contract income is reported under one of the two methods:

(1) Percentage of completion method, or
(2) Percentage of completion-capitalized cost method. Under this new method, a taxpayer must account for 40 percent of the items related to the contract under the percentage of completion method. Percentage of completion is determined by comparing the total contract costs incurred before the close of the taxable year with the estimated total contract costs; the remaining 60 percent is accounted for under the taxpayer's normal method of accounting. Thus, 60 percent of the gross contract income is reported, and 60 percent of the contract costs are deducted following the taxpayer's regular method of reporting. A look-back method applies to 40 percent of the contract reported on the percentage of completion.

Independent research and development costs incurred in a long-term contract are allocable to the contract.

Small construction contract exception. The new rules do not apply to small construction real estate contracts if the contract (1) is expected to be completed within the two-year period beginning on the first date of the contract, and (2) is performed by a taxpayer whose average annual gross receipts do not exceed $10 million for the three taxable years before the taxable year of the execution of the contract.

The new law applies generally to contracts entered into after February 28, 1986.

CANCELLATION OF BUSINESS DEBT

Under prior law, a solvent debtor could elect to defer income arising from the discharge of a business debt. This rule is repealed. After 1986, income from the discharge of any debt is taxable unless the discharge occurs in a title 11 (Bankruptcy) proceeding or when the debtor is insolvent.

ALLOCATING THE PURCHASE PRICE OF A BUSINESS

A purchase of a business involves the purchase of various individual business assets of the business. Under prior law, the seller would generally assign a larger portion of the sales price to capital assets to such as goodwill to realize capital gain. The buyer would assign a larger part of the same price to inventory and deductible costs items in order to get larger current deductions. To force buyer and sellers to follow the same allocation rules, the new law requires both the buyer and the seller to allocate the purchase price of a business among the transferred assets using a residual basis formula.

The new law applies to an "applicable asset acquisition" which is a sale of a group of assets considered a business in which the bases of assets of the business are determined by the price paid for the business. A group of assets is considered a business if their character is such that goodwill or going concern value could under any circumstances attach to the assets. Goodwill is the excess of the purchase price over the aggregate fair market values of the tangible assets and the identifiable intangible assets other than goodwill. The residual method is explained in Temporary Reg. Sec. 1.338 (b)-2T for allocating the purchase price of stock to assets in the company.

The new law applies to transactions after May 6, 1986, except for a transaction made under a contract binding on and after that date.

EXTENDED DEDUCTION
PASSTHROUGH OF CO-OP APARTMENTS
TAXES AND INTEREST

A tenant-stockholder of a cooperative may deduct his share of payments made by the corporation for mortgage interest and real estate taxes. Under prior law, only individuals were generally entitled to the passthrough deduction. The new law extends the deduction to corporations, estates, and other entities that own cooperative units. If a business claims depreciation, the depreciation deductions may not exceed the basis of the stock. Amounts not deductible because of the basis limitation may be carried forward to later years and deducted if stock basis allocated to depreciable property exceeds zero.

The new rules apply to taxable years beginning after 1986.

BUSINESS ENERGY
CREDITS EXTENDED

The following business credits are allowed under the new law:

For	Percentage	Placed In
Solar Energy	15%	1986
	12%	1987
	10%	1988
Geothermal	15%	1986
	10%	1987-1988
Ocean Thermal	15%	1986-1988
Biomass	15%	1986
	10%	1987

Under prior law, these business energy credits were to expire at the end of 1985. The individual residential energy credit was allowed to expire at the end of 1985.

RESEARCH AND DEVELOPMENT CREDIT EXTENDED

The new law renews the R&D credit for three years, but it reduces the credit from 25 percent to 20 percent. Expenditures eligible for the credit are costs incurred to discover technological information that results in a new item for sale or use in a company's business.

LOW-INCOME HOUSING TAX CREDIT

Under prior law, low-income housing was depreciable over 15 years. This tax benefit may not generally be claimed for property placed in service after 1986. In its place, the new law provides three tax credits for low-income housing placed in service after 1986 and before 1990. The new credits are claimed over a 10-year period. For new constructed and rehabilitated property placed in service in 1987, the annual credit is nine percent. But if construction is financed with tax-exempt bonds or similar Federal subsidies, the credit is four percent. Expenditures must exceed $2,000 per unit.

A credit of four percent applies to the costs of acquiring existing low-income housing which has not been previously placed in service within 10 years.

REHABILITATION TAX CREDIT MODIFIED

Under prior law, there was a three-level investment tax credit of 15 percent to 25 percent for the expenses of rehabilitating old buildings and certified historic structures.

Under the new law, there is a 20 percent credit for rehabilitating certified historic structures and a 10 percent credit for rehabilitation costs of buildings, other than historic structures, built before 1936.

Rehabilitation credit for historic structures applies to both residential and nonresidential buildings: The credit for nonhistoric buildings applies only to nonresidential buildings.

The basis of the building is reduced by the full amount of the credit taken.

The new credits apply to property placed in service after 1986. Transitional rules are not discussed in this book.

REMOVAL OF ARCHITECTURAL BARRIERS TO THE HANDICAPPED AND ELDERLY

Under the new law, a deduction is allowed of up to $35,000 for costs incurred to remove architectural and transportation barriers to the handicapped and elderly. Under prior law, the deduction was allowed only for expenses incurred in taxable years beginning before 1986.

TRADEMARK AND TRADE NAME AMORTIZATION REPEALED

Under prior law, there was an election to amortize over 60 months expenditures for acquiring, protecting, expanding, registering, or defending a trademark or trade name. The new law repeals the election. Trademarks and trade name expenditures are added to the basis of assets to which they relate and recovered when the asset is disposed of.

The repeal affects expenditures paid or incurred after 1986. Under a transition rule, the amortization election may apply to expenditures incurred (1) pursuant to a written contract binding as of March 1, 1986; or (2) for developing, protecting, expanding, registering, or defending trademarks or trade names begun as of March 1, 1986, if the lesser of $1 million or five percent of the cost has been incurred or committed by that date. The trademark or trade name must be placed in service before 1988.

CORPORATE TAX CHANGES

Corporate tax rates reduced.   The five graduated tax rates are replaced by three rates and the top corporate tax rate is lowered from 46 percent to 34 percent as follows:

If taxable income is—	Tax rate is—
Not over $50,000	15%
Over $50,000 but not over $75,000	25%
Over $75,000	34%

For taxable income over $100,000, an additional 5 percent tax is applied; however, this tax surcharge may not exceed $11,750. That is, the benefit of graduated rates for corporations with taxable incomes between $100,000 and $335,000 is phased out. Corporations with income in excess of $335,000 pay an effective flat tax at a 34 percent rate.

The above tax rates are effective for tax years beginning on or after July 1, 1987. For fiscal years that straddle July 1, 1987, prior-year and the new rates are blended.

Corporate alternative capital tax repealed.   Under pre-1987 law, a 28 percent alternative tax rate applies to corporate net capital gain. Under the new law, the alternative tax rate for net capital gains is repealed for taxable years beginning on or after July 1, 1987. A special alternative capital gains tax may apply to a fiscal tax year that began before January 1, 1987. The alternative tax in that case is a blend of the 28 percent alternative rate of prior law for 1986 gains and the new law maximum 34 percent rate for 1987 gains. For taxable years starting after 1986 but before July 1, 1987, the alternative rate is 34 percent. For the application of these rules you must follow IRS tax return instructions.

Important: The new law keeps the statutory structure for capital gains to facilitate reinstatement of a capital gains rate differential if there is a future tax rate increase.

Corporate alternative minimum tax.   Under pre-1987 law, there was a corporate additional minimum tax with a 15 percent tax rate. Starting in 1987, the new law applies a corporate AMT similar to the individual AMT. A corporate AMT must also make estimated tax payments based on AMT tax. The new corporate AMT rate is 20 percent. The exemption is $40,000, up from $10,000 with phaseout beginning at $150,000 of taxable income at a rate of 25 cents for every dollar over $150,000; the exemption ends at $310,000. Controlled groups must apportion the exemption. Corporate preference items are not discussed in this book.

Corporate dividends-received deduction decreased.   The corporate dividends-received deduction is reduced to 80 percent from 85 percent for regular dividends received by corporations, dividends received on certain preferred stock, and dividends on debt-financed portfolio stock.

The new law also changes holding period rules for extraordinary dividends.

Stock redemption expenses not deductible. Under a new law, a corporation may not deduct expenses related to the redemption of its stock. The new rule is aimed at deductions claimed for ''greenmail'' payments in hostile takeovers. However, the disallowance rule applies to all stock redemptions. The nondeductible rule applies to such payments for repurchase of stock, premiums paid for the stock, and legal, accounting, brokerage, transfer agent, appraisal, and similar fees related to the redemption.

The disallowance rule also does not apply to costs incurred by a mutual fund in processing redemption applications and issuing checks to pay for redeemed shares. It also does not apply to personal holding companies, foreign personal holding company taxes, and real estate investment trusts.

Limitations on acquisition carryover losses. To reduce the appeal of acquiring companies for their carryovers, the new law sets down new restrictions. After a change in corporate ownership, prior net operating losses are deductible only within the framework of a formula based on the value of the corporation before the change. A change in ownership occurs if the percentage of stock of the new loss corporation owned by any one or more five percent shareholders has increased by more than 50 percentage points relative to the lowest percentage of stock owned by those five percent shareholders during a period of three years before the change of ownership. The period may not start before May 6, 1986.

REPEAL OF STATUTES ALLOWING TAX-FREE CORPORATE LIQUIDATION DISTRIBUTIONS AND 12-MONTH LIQUIDATIONS

Under prior law, a corporation (1) realized no gain or loss on distribution of property in a complete liquidation (Section 336), and (2) could adopt a special 12-month liquidation and sell appreciated assets without tax and then distribute proceeds in liquidation. Tax was incurred only by stockholders depending on the value of the distribution and the cost basis of their stock.

The new law repeals those two basic tax provisions.

With the repeal, a corporation is taxed on distribution of appreciated property. Further, there is no longer any tax shelter for corporate sales of property in a 12-month corporate liquidation as allowed under prior Section 337. Under the new law, gain or loss is generally recognized by a corporation on a liquidating sale of its assets and gain or loss is also generally recognized to a corporation on a distribution of its property in complete liquidation. The distributing corporation is treated as if it had sold the property to the distributee-shareholders at fair market value. However, gain or loss is not recognized for any distribution of property by a corporation to the extent the tax-free reorganization rules apply.

If the distributed property is subject to a liability, or the shareholders assume liabilities, the value of the asset may not be less than the amount of the liability. Gain is generally taxable to the extent the liability exceeds basis.

Nonliquidating distributions are treated the same as liquidating distributions. Gain is recognized to the distributing corporation if appreciated property other than the corporate obligations is distributed to shareholders.

The new law also repeals prior law exceptions for tax-free treatment for nonliquidating distributions to noncorporate shareholders, and for distributions of property relating to the payment of estate taxes or certain redemptions of private foundation stock.

Effect on S election.   S elections by a C corporation are subject to a new "built-in" gain rule. Where a C corporation makes an S corporation election, appreciation on assets is kept in suspense for 10 years. A tax is triggered on the S corporation if within the 10-year period it disposes of the gain property. The new rule does not apply if the corporation can show that the asset was not held when the corporation was a C corporation, or the gain is attributable to appreciation occurring after the S election.

Complete liquidations of subsidiaries.   When a subsidiary is completely liquidated into its parent, no gain or loss may be recognized on the distribution. Tax may be incurred if the parent corporation later disposes of the property to an outsider. Tax-free rules apply if the distributee corporation meets at least the 80 percent ownership test. If a minority shareholder receives property, gain but not loss is recognized. Tax may also be incurred by a parent tax-exempt organization, unless the property received in the distribution is used in an unrelated business after the distribution. If the property later is not so used, the tax is imposed.

A corporate buyer and a seller of an 80 percent-controlled subsidiary may elect to treat the sale of the subsidiary stock as if the underlying assets were sold. The selling corporation and the target subsidiary must be members of an affiliated group filing a consolidated return for the tax year that includes the acquisition date. If an election is made, the underlying assets of the company that are sold may be valued at fair market value.

The new law covering liquidations applies generally to distribution in complete liquidation and any sale or exchange made by a corporation after July 31, 1986, unless the corporation is completely liquidated before 1987 and to distributions not in complete liquidation made after 1986. There is also a transitional rule. The new law does not apply to distributions or sales made under a liquidation plan adopted before August 1, 1986. Transactions are treated as made under a pre-August 1, 1986 plan if before November 20, 1985, the company adopted a resolution to get shareholder approval for a distribution or liquidation, or the deal was approved by the shareholders or directors. The old law also applies if before that date there was an offer to buy a majority of the liquidating corporation voting stock, or a resolution recommending or approving an acquisition was adopted, or a ruling request was submitted to the IRS. In these cases, sales and distributions must be completed before January 1, 1988.

Under special rules, prior law rules for liquidations are partially retained for small, closely held companies on liquidating sales or distributions occurring before January 1, 1989, if the liquidation is completed by that date. However, gain or loss must be recognized on distribution of ordinary income property and short-term capital gain property.

OPERATING AS AN S CORPORATION

The legal advantages of a corporation are available without the payment of corporate tax. By filing an S election to report corporate earnings and losses, you may keep the election as long as it benefits you or for as short a period as one year. As a stockholder, you agree to report on your personal tax return your share of the corporation's undistributed taxable income as ordinary income.

Items of income, deductions, losses, and credits of the corporation pass through to the shareholders in the same general manner as the character of such items of a partnership passes through to partners. Thus, for example, such items as tax-exempt interest and gains and losses on the sale of the corporation pass through and retain their character in the hands of shareholders.

An S election may be advisable for a new corporation which anticipates losses at the start. The shareholders may deduct their share of these losses on their personal tax returns.

S corporations are also advisable when the corporate rates for regular C corporations are higher than the top personal tax rates for stockholders. In 1988, the scheduled top rate for C corporations is 34 percent while the top personal rate is 28 percent. Under this rate structure, an S corporation is a better choice, especially since retained earnings later distributed by a C corporation are subject to ordinary income tax when received by stockholders. This is true even though the earnings were previously subject to corporate tax. Thus an S corporation avoids a double tax on earnings. For example in 1988, earnings of an S corporation reported by a stockholder would be subject to a 28 percent rate whereas in the C corporation it might first be subject to a corporate tax ranging from 15 percent to 34 percent and the balance of the earnings when distributed to the stockholder subject to a personal tax of up to 28 percent.

Warning: If an S election is made by a C corporation, that is, one already in existence and subject to regular corporation tax, the S corporation may have to pay tax on the sale of appreciated property held by the company before the election. The gain must be reported by the S corporation if the property is sold or distributed within 10 years of the date of the S election. The new rule applies to elections made after December 31, 1986, but not to S elections made before or on that date. Also consider the loss of certain fringe benefits to employee stockholders if an election is made.

YEAR-END STOCK SALES MAY NOT BE DEFERRED TO NEXT YEAR

Under pre-1987 law, it is possible under the installment sale rule to execute a sale of stock on the public exchange at the end of the year and defer the reporting of gain until the next year. Starting in 1987, gains are recognized on the day the trade is executed, even though cash is not received until the next year. Under both prior and new law, losses are deductible in the year of the sale.

REVISED
DEPRECIATION
RULES

RAPID DEPRECIATION ENCOURAGED BY THE TAX LAW

Depreciation is an expense deduction that allows you to charge off your capital investments in equipment, machines, fixtures, autos, trucks, and buildings used in your business, profession, or rental or other income-producing activities.

The law encourages accelerated writeoffs over short periods of time through one of the following methods or a combination of both.

Accelerated Cost Recovery System (ACRS). The objective of ACRS is to provide rapid depreciation for most asset purchases and to eliminate disputes over useful life, salvage value, and depreciation methods. Useful life and depreciation methods are fixed by ACRS; salvage value is not considered. If you do not want to use the rates fixed by ACRS, you may elect an alternative depreciation which is basically the straight line method. ACRS applies to new and used property. Except for certain railroad property not discussed in this book, the ACRS rules do not apply to property for which an election is made to claim depreciation under a method not expressed in terms of years, such as the unit-of-production or income forecast methods.

First-year expensing. This is a one-time deduction up to certain fixed amounts. It allows you to deduct all or part of the cost of business equipment bought in a taxable year instead of depreciating the asset over the applicable ACRS period. First-year expensing does not apply to buildings or property used in the production of income.

What property may be depreciated?   Depreciation may be claimed only on property used in your business or other income-producing activity. Depreciation may not be claimed on property held for personal purposes, such as a personal residence or pleasure car. If property, such as a car, is used for both business and pleasure, only the business portion may be depreciated.

Property bought for income-producing purposes, although yielding no current income, may still be depreciated.

Not all assets used in your business or for the production of income may be depreciable. Property having no determinable useful life (property that will never be used up or become obsolete) such as treasured art works or goodwill, may not be depreciated. Although land is not depreciable, the cost of landscaping business property may be depreciated.

Property held primarily for sale to customers or property includible in inventory is not depreciable, regardless of its useful life.

Depreciation is deducted annually. Even though the deduction may give you no tax benefit in a particular year because your other deductions already exceed your income, you may not choose to forego the depreciation deduction and, instead, accumulate it for high income years. Similarly, incorrect deductions claimed in prior years may not be corrected by an adjustment to your present depreciation deduction. If the year in which the error was made is not yet closed by the statute of limitations, you may file an amended return to adjust the depreciation deduction for that year.

NEW LAW CHANGES
MADE TO DEPRECIATION

The new law makes the following changes for assets placed in service after 1986:

> *Restructures some ACRS class life qualifications.* Business autos and light trucks are removed from the three-year class life and placed in a five-year class life. Office furniture and fixtures are removed from the five-year class and placed in a new seven-year class. The recovery period for real estate is increased from 19 years to 27.5 years for residential rental property and to 31.5 years for non-residential property.

Replaces ACRS rate percentages with double-declining method for class lives of three, five, seven, and ten years.

Sets a mid-year convention and mid-quarter conventions for the first year of acquisition. Generally, regardless of the placement date, only 50 percent of the annual deduction is allowed in the first year. Consequently, the effective writeoff period for three-year life is four years, five-year life is six years, seven-year life is eight years. However, a mid-quarter convention may apply where asset acquisitions in the last three months are at least 40 percent of total acquisitions during the year. In such a case, a mid-quarter convention replaces the mid-year convention.

Increases the first-year expensing deduction from $5,000 to $10,000. However, if the cost of qualifying assets exceeds $200,000, the limit is reduced dollar-for-dollar by the cost of payments exceeding $200,000.

The imposition of the new system complicates depreciation calculation. Depending on when they were placed in service, assets may be depreciated under pre-1981 depreciation rules, the original ACRS rules for assets placed in service from 1981-1986, and the new ACRS rules for assets placed in service after 1986.

NEW CLASS LIVES

Depreciable assets (other than buildings) fall within a three, five, seven, 10, 15, or 20-year class life. For property in the three, four, seven- and 10-year classes, the depreciation method is 200 percent declining balance, with a switch to straight line. For 15- and 20-year property, the 150 percent declining balance is used with a switch to straight line. The conversion to straight line is made when larger annual deductions may be claimed over the remaining life.

Three-year property.   This class includes property with a four-year-or-less midpoint life under the ADR (Asset Depreciation Range) system, other than cars and light-duty trucks (which are in the five-year class).

Property with a midpoint life of four years or less includes: Special handling devices for the manufacture of food and beverages; special tools and devices for the manufacture of rubber products; special tools for the manufacture of finished plastic products, fabricated metal products, or motor vehicles; and breeding hogs. By law, racehorses more than two years old when placed in service and other horses more than 12 years old when placed in service, are also in the three-year class.

Five-year class.   This includes property with an ADR midpoint of more than four years and less than 10 years, such as computers, typewriters, copiers, duplicating equipment, heavy general purpose trucks, trailers, cargo containers, and trailer-mounted containers. Also included by law in the five-year class are cars, light-duty trucks, computer-based telephone central office switching equipment, computer related peripheral equipment, semiconductor manufacturing equipment, and property used in research and experimentation.

Seven-year property.   This is a new class and includes any property with an ADR midpoint of 10 years or more and less than 16 years, and property with no ADR midpoint that is not assigned to another class. In this class are: Office furniture, fixtures and equipment (formerly in the five-year class), railroad track, and single-purpose agricultural and horticultural structures.

Ten-year property.   This includes property with an ADR midpoint of 16 years or more and less than 20 years (generally assets used in petroleum refining, or in the manufacture of tobacco products and certain food products).

Fifteen-year property.   This includes property with an ADR midpoint of 20 years or more and less than 25 years, such as municipal sewage treatment plants, telephone distribution plants, and comparable equipment used by nontelephone companies for the two-way exchange of voice and data communications.

Twenty-year property. This is a new class and includes property with an ADR midpoint of 25 years and more, other than Sec. 1250 real property with an ADR midpoint of 27.5 years and more.

DECLINING
BALANCE METHOD

Under the declining balance method, depreciation deductions are largest in the first year and decrease each year thereafter. The actual deduction is figured by increasing the straight line rate by a percentage and then applying that percentage to the cost basis of the asset. Under the double or 200 percent declining balance rate, the straight line rate is doubled. For example, if the straight line rate for five-year property is 20 percent, the double declining rate is 40 percent. Normally the 40 percent rate is applied to the declining cost basis after adjusting for prior depreciation. When the declining rate provides a lower annual deduction than the straight line rate, the double declining rate is replaced by the straight line rate. Under the new ACRS rules, these general rules are modified because of the mid-year and mid-quarter conventions. Under the mid-year convention, all property acquired during the year, regardless of when acquired during the year, is treated as acquired in the middle of the year. As a result, only one half of the first-year depreciation is deductible and in the year after the last class life year, the balance of the depreciation is written off. Further, in the year property is sold, only half of the depreciation of that year is deductible. Under the original ACRS system, no depreciation was allowed in the year property was disposed of. A mid-month convention applies to real estate.

The following is a table of rates reflecting the mid-year convention and a straight line conversion to the year marked by asterisks. For purposes of convenience, the rates have been adjusted for the mid-year convention and are applied against original basis of the asset, rather than the declining basis. The adjusted rate reflects the application of the rate to the declining balance. The rates are not official.

Recovery Year	3-Year	5-Year	7-Year
1	33.00%	20.00%	14.28%
2	45.00%	32.00%	24.49%
3	15.00%*	19.20%	17.49%
4	7.00%	11.52%*	12.49*
5		11.52%	8.93%*
6		5.76%	8.93%
7			8.93%
8			4.46%

Do not apply these percentages if a mid-quarter convention applies.
* Year of switch to straight line method.

For illustrative purposes only, the following is a table showing five-year declining balance rates if no conventions applied. The effect of the mid-year convention can be seen by comparing the following rates without the convention with the above chart which includes the legally required convention.

(Illustrative)

Five-Year Declining Balance	Full Years No Conventions
Year	Rate
1	40%
2	24%
3	14.4%
4	10.8%
5	10.8%

FINAL QUARTER ASSET PLACEMENTS—MID-QUARTER CONVENTIONS

A mid-quarter convention applies if the total cost bases of property placed in service during the last three months of the tax year exceed 40 percent of the total bases of all the property placed in service during the year. You must use a mid-quarter convention for *all property* (other than nonresidential real property and residential rental property) placed in service during the year. In applying the 40 percent rule, you do not count residential rental property and non-residential realty.

Under the mid-quarter convention, the first-year depreciation allowance is based on the number of quarters that the asset was in service. Property placed in service at any time during a quarter is treated as having been placed in service in the middle of the quarter.

Members of an affiliated group may be treated as one taxpayer for purposes of the 40 percent test.

EXAMPLE—

Assume the mid-quarter asset convention applies. For five-year class property costing $100 and placed in service during the first quarter of a taxable year, the deductions beginning in the first taxable year are $35, second $26, third $15.60, fourth $11.10, fifth $11.01 and sixth $1.38.

Five-Year Declining Balance Mid-Quarter Convention

Year	1st Quarter	2nd Quarter	3rd Quarter	4th Quarter
			Rate is	
1	35%	25%	15%	5%
2	26	30	34	38
4	15.6	18	20.4	22.8
4	11.01	11.37	11.66	11.9
5	11.01	11.37	11.66	11.9
6	1.38	4.26	7.28	10.4

Important: The above figures are not official and are presented for purposes of illustration.

For the taxable year in which property is placed in service subject both to pre-1987 ACRS and to post-1986 ACRS, the 40-percent determination is on the basis of all property acquisition. The mid-quarter convention, however, applies only to property subject to post-1986 ACRS rules.

ALTERNATIVE DEPRECIATION

You may not want to use an accelerated rate and may prefer to write off depreciation at an even pace. You may elect to use the alternative depreciation which is the straight-line method (without regard to salvage value) and using one of the following recovery periods fixed by law.

For	The recovery period is
Cars and light trucks	5 years
Personal property with no class life	12 years
Nonresidential real and residential real property	40 years
Other property	class life

Except for real estate, straight-line election applies to all property within the same class. For real estate, the election to use this straight-line method may be made on a property by property basis.

The alternative method must also be used to determine the amount of tax preferences arising for ACRS depreciation for purposes of alternative minimum tax. Also for AMT purposes, accelerated depreciation rate for personal property is 150 percent declining balance.

You are also required to use the alternative depreciation system for—

Figuring earnings and profits,
Any tangible property which during the taxable year is used predominantly outside the United States,
Any tax-exempt use property,
Any tax-exempt bond financed property,
Any imported property covered by an Executive order.

Instead of the above alternative method, you may elect the straight-line method over the regular recovery period.

Mid-year and quarter-year conventions apply to alternative method depreciations.

The alternative rate for five-year property assuming a mid-year convention is as follows:

Year	Rate
1	10
2	20
3	20
4	20
5	20
6	10

The alternative rate for 40-year realty during the second to 40th year is 2½ percent. The rates for the first year and the 41st year depend on months the property was placed in service; these rates are listed in Treasury regulations.

ELECTION FOR ASSETS PLACED IN SERVICE AFTER JULY 31, 1986

You may elect the new ACRS rules for assets placed in service after July 31, 1986, and before January 1, 1987. You may want to consider the election for assets that have not been transferred to a longer ACRS class. In such a case, the application of double declining rates may give larger deductions in the first two years than provided by the original ACRS rate (see example below). The election should not be made for assets transferred into a longer recovery class, such as automobiles.

EXAMPLE—

You buy a photocopy machine in August 1986 costing $10,000. Under both ACRS systems, the class life is five years. However, the deduction amounts over the recovery period differ. Assume the mid-year convention applies under new law.

Year	Original ACRS	New ACRS
1	$1,500	$2,000
2	2,200	3,200
3	2,100	1,920
4	2,100	1,152
5	2,100	1,152
6	—	576

GENERAL RULES
FOR CLAIMING DEPRECIATION
ON AN AUTO

All autos placed in service after June 18, 1984 are subject to a business use test, recapture rules, and annual ceilings on depreciation.

More than 50 percent business use test. Whether you are an employee or are self employed, you may claim ACRS for a car bought after June 18, 1984, only if you use it more than 50 percent of the time for business in the year you place it in service.

If business use is 50 percent or less in the year the car is placed in service, ACRS is barred; the auto is depreciable under an alternative method, which is basically the straight-line method over six years, subject also to the mid-year or mid-quarter convention.

If a car is used for both business and investment purposes, only business use is considered under the more than 50 percent business use test to determine the right to claim ACRS and/or first-year expensing. However, if business use exceeds 50 percent, investment use is added to business use when determining the depreciable percentage.

Recapture of ACRS if business use falls below 51 percent. If you meet the more than 50 percent test in the year the car is placed in service but business falls to 50 percent or less in a later year, there is recapture of depreciation.

Employer convenience test.   If you are an employee and use your own car for work, you must be ready to prove that you use a car for the convenience of your employer who requires you to use it in your job. If you do not meet this employer convenience test, you may not use ACRS, including the elective straight-line method. A letter from your employer stating you need the car for business will not be enough to meet this test.

The facts and circumstances of your use of the car may show that it is a condition of employment. For example, an inspector for a construction company uses his automobile to visit construction sites over a scattered area. The company reimburses him for his expenses. According to the IRS, the inspector's use of the car is for the convenience of the company and is a condition of the job. However, if a company car were available to the inspector, the use of his own car would not meet the condition of employment and convenience of the employer tests.

For a car placed in service after April 2, 1985, and before 1987, the ACRS deduction in the first year is limited to $3,200; in the second year and third year the deduction may not exceed $4,800 each year. If in the first three years business use is 100 percent, then any remaining basis that could not be deducted because of the $3,200 and $4,800 ceilings may be depreciated at a rate of up to $4,800 a year until basis is written off.

Personal use.   Where a deduction is limited by the ceiling and the car is also used for personal driving, the business use percentage is applied to the ceiling. For example, in 1986 you buy a car costing $40,000. ACRS is limited by the $3,200 ceiling. You use the car 80 percent for business travel. The ACRS deduction is limited to $2,560 ($3,200 x 80%).

DEPRECIATING A BUSINESS AUTO IN 1987 AND LATER YEARS

Business autos placed in service in 1987 and later years are technically in a five-year class but are actually depreciated over a six-year period because of the mid-year or mid-quarter convention. The ACRS rate is based on 200 percent declining balance method with a switchover to straight line. However, the full amount of the deduction is not allowed because of annual so-called luxury car limits. The new limits are—

Year	Annual limit is—
1	$2,560
2	4,100
3	2,450
4	1,475
5	1,475
6	1,475

Combining the above annual limits with the depreciation rates applied to the original depreciable basis of the car your annual deduction will be as follows under the mid-year convention—

Year	Lower of—
1	20% or $2,560
2	32% or $4,100
3	19.20% or $2,450
4	11.52% or $1,475
5	11.52% or $1,475
6	5.76% or $1,475

EXAMPLES—

1. In 1987, you place in service a car used 100 percent in business. The car cost $20,000. Here is the depreciation schedule assuming the car is kept for the period shown below:

1987	$2,560
1988	4,100
1989	2,450
1990	1,475
1991	1,475
1992	1,152
1993	1,475

1994	1,475
1995	1,475
1996	1,475
1997	888

2. Assume you use the car only 60 percent for business. You deduct $1,536 in 1987 which is 60 percent of the annual limit of $2,560. Your deduction may not be based on 60 percent of depreciable basis; this would give a larger deduction of $2,400 ($20,000 x 60 percent x 20 percent) without considering the relative range of the annual luxury car limit.

Important: If a car is put in service at the end of a taxable year, the first-year deduction may be limited by a mid-quarter convention.

REAL ESTATE DEPRECIATION

The new law increases the recovery period for buildings placed in service after December 31, 1986. It is 27.5 years for residential rental property and 31.5 years for nonresidential real property. The method of recovery is the straight-line rate using a mid-month convention. The annual rate for years two through 27 for residential property is 3.64 percent and for nonresidential the rate for years two through 31 is 3.17 percent. The first and last year rate varies with the month placed in service.

Residential rental property is property that provides at least 80 percent of the gross rental income from dwelling units. Residential rental property does not include hotels, motels, and other units rented to transients. Nonresidential real property is a building that is not residential rental property and that either has no ADR midpoint or has an ADR midpoint that is not less than 27½ years. Because of the mid-month convention no depreciation adjustment is necessary for short tax years.

You may elect to use the straight-line method (and the mid-month convention) over a 40-year period.

Under the new law, if a building is erected on leased property, the cost of the building must be recovered over the 27½ year (residential year) period or 31½ year (nonresidential) period, regardless of the lease term. The cost of other improvements to leased property is recovered using the applicable ACRS recovery period.

ACRS RESTRICTIONS

ACRS under the post-1986 rates does not apply to personal property acquired after 1986 if (1) you, a family member, or other related persons, owned or used it during 1986, or (2) you or a related person leased the property during 1986. In such cases, pre-1987 ACRS rules apply. The above restriction does not apply to: (1) real estate, (2) property used for personal purposes before 1987 and converted to business use after 1986, and (3) when pre-1987 ACRS rules would give a larger deduction than the post-1986 rules. For example, you use a business auto during 1986 and then transfer it to your son in 1987. Your son must use the 1987 ACRS rule.

INCREASED FIRST-YEAR EXPENSING DEDUCTION

Starting in 1987, you may elect to treat all or part of the cost of business equipment as a currently deductible expense up to $10,000. Before 1987, the deduction was limited to $5,000. You will make the election if you want a larger deduction in the year you place the asset in service than the deduction provided by ACRS depreciation.

The new law also sets these limits:

(1) If the total cost of qualifying property placed in service during a taxable year is over $200,000, the $10,000 limit is reduced dollar-for-dollar by the cost of qualifying property exceeding $200,000.

(2) The deduction may not exceed the total taxable income
from all businesses which you actively conduct. Taxable income from business is computed without regard
to the amount expensed. If qualified costs exceed taxable income, the cost may be carried forward to the next
tax year and added to expenses in that year.

If a married couple files separate returns, the $10,000 expensing
limit and the $200,000 cost limit for qualifying property applies to
both taxpayers as a unit. Unless they elect otherwise, 50 percent of
the cost of qualifying property is allocated to each spouse.

TRANSITIONAL RULES
FOR DEPRECIATION
AND INVESTMENT CREDIT

The new depreciation rules generally apply for assets placed in
service after 1986.

The investment credit has generally been repealed for assets
placed in service after 1985. However, under transition rules, prior
law depreciation and the investment credit may still be available.
You may apply 1986 depreciation rules for assets placed in service
after 1986 if acquired or constructed under contracts binding as of
March 1, 1986, the property has a class life of at least seven years,
and it is placed in service by a specified cutoff date. For example, in
the case of real estate, residential or nonresidential, the building
must be placed in service before January 1, 1991, to qualify for 19-
year depreciation under 1986 rules.

The transition rule for the investment credit applies to property
that was subject to a binding contract as of December 31, 1985, but
only if the property was placed in service by a specific cutoff date.
For property with a class life of less than five years, such as a
business auto, the property had to be placed in service before July 1,
1986, to qualify for the credit under the transition rule. If the class
life for business equipment is at least five years but less than seven
years, and it was subject to a binding contract on December 31,

1985, a 1986 investment credit may be claimed if the property is placed in service before January 1, 1987. The cutoff date is January 1, 1989, for equipment with a class life of at least seven but less than 20 years; or January 1, 1991 for equipment with a class life of 20 years or more.

These are the general transition rules. There are other numerous transition rules for specific investment projects.

If the credit may be claimed, these new limitations will apply: Credits and carryovers of prior year credits must be reduced by 35 percent for tax years starting on or after July 1, 1987. For calendar year taxpayers, the 1987 reduction is 17.5 percent. The portion of the credit subject to the reduction is lost forever. Further, basis for depreciation purposes must be reduced by 100 percent of the credit instead of 50 percent as under current law. Further, you have no option to avoid the basis reduction by electing a lower credit percentage, as under current law.

FARM, TIMBER, ENERGY, AND NATURAL RESOURCES

SOIL AND WATER
CONSERVATION EXPENDITURES

Under prior law, a farmer may elect to deduct certain expenditures made for the purpose of soil or water conservation that otherwise would be required to be capitalized. Expenditures eligible for the election are costs of grading, terracing, contour furrowing, construction of drainage ditches, irrigation ditches, dams and ponds, and planting of windbreaks.

The annual deduction is limited to 25 percent of gross income from farming.

Under the new law, soil and water conservation expenditures incurred or paid after 1986 are eligible for the expensing election only if the expenditures are consistent with a conservation plan approved by the Soil Conservation Service of the Department of Agriculture, or in the absence of such a plan, a plan of a comparable state conservation agency. While prior approval of a particular project is not necessary to qualify the expenditure, there must be an approved overall plan for the area in effect at any time during the taxable year. The expensing election does not apply to expenditures for draining or filling of wetlands or preparing land for installation or operation of a center pivot irrigation system.

CAPITAL GAIN RULES RETAINED
FOR CERTAIN 1987 SALES
OF DAIRY CATTLE

Prior law capital gains rules apply to gains from sales of dairy cattle to the U.S. Department of Agriculture under its milk production termination program provided the gain is realized (under the taxpayer's accounting method) after January 1, 1987, and before September 1, 1987. For such sales, the prior law capital gains deduction for individuals, and the prior law alternative tax rate for corporate capital gains will continue to apply.

DISPOSITION OF
CONVERTED WETLANDS
OR ERODIBLE CROPLAND

Under the new law, gain on the disposition of wetlands or highly erodible cropland converted to farming use is treated as ordinary income. Any loss on the disposition of such property is treated as a long-term capital loss. These rules apply to dispositions of land converted to farming use after March 1, 1986. Converted wetlands is such land within the meaning of the 1985 Food Security Act.

LAND CLEARING EXPENDITURES
ELECTION REPEALED

Under prior law, a farmer may elect to deduct current land clearing expenditures incurred for the purpose of making such land suitable for farming. For any taxable year, the deduction may not exceed the lesser of $5,000 or 25 percent of the taxable farm income.

Under new law, the election to expense land clearing expenditures is repealed for expenditures after December 31, 1985.

PRE-PAYMENT
OF FARMING EXPENSES

Under prior law, farmers generally may use the cash method of accounting and deduct prepayments of farm expenses. However, a farming syndicate may not deduct any amount paid for feed, seed, or other similar supplies prior to the year in which such supplies are used or consumed.

Under the new law, farmers other than qualifying full-time farmers using the cash method may not deduct amounts paid for unconsumed feed, seed, fertilizer, or other supplies to the extent they exceed 50 percent of total expenses incurred in the farming business during the taxable year, excluding prepaid expenses. A similar rule applies in the case of costs incurred for the purchase of poultry. The provision is effective for prepayments made on or after March 1, 1986, in taxable years beginning after that date.

DISCHARGE
OF FARM INDEBTEDNESS

Under prior law, if a business debt is discharged by a creditor, income is not realized if an election to reduce basis in depreciable property is made. If the amount of the indebtedness forgiven exceeds basis, income is recognized to the extent of the excess. If debt of an insolvent taxpayer is discharged, the taxpayer may exclude the income to the extent of insolvency. Net operating loss carryovers (and investment credit carryovers) and basis in property may be reduced by the amount of the excluded income. However, the aggregate basis in assets may not be reduced below the amount of the remaining undischarged liabilities. If the discharge of indebtedness income exceeds the taxpayer's available tax attributes and basis, tax on the excess is forgiven.

Under a new law, income from a discharge of indebtedness owed by a qualifying farmer to an unrelated lender is treated as income realized by an insolvent taxpayer, if the debt was incurred in farming or is farm business debt secured by farmland or farm equipment used in such trade business. You are eligible for this relief only if 50 percent or more of your average annual gross receipts for the preceding three taxable years was derived from farming. The provision is effective for discharges of indebtedness after April 9, 1986.

PREPRODUCTIVE PERIOD
EXPENSES OF FARMERS

Individual farmers may elect to use the cash method of accounting when the accrual method otherwise would be required. They may use simplified inventory methods if an accrual method is adopted. Most farmers use the cash method of accounting, and therefore do not keep inventories or capitalize preproductive period costs. Costs incurred in planting, cultivating, maintaining, or developing citrus or almond groves before the end of the fourth taxable year after planting must be capitalized. Farming syndicates must capitalize planting and maintenance costs incurred in orchard, grove, or vineyard crops until production in commercial quantities begins. However, if an orchard, grove, or vineyard is lost or damaged by reason of freezing temperatures, drought, disease, pests, or casualty, otherwise deductible replanting and maintenance costs are currently deductible if the same property is replanted.

Under a new law, farmers must generally capitalize costs incurred after 1986 for producing plants or raising animals with a preproductive period of more than two years. However, an election to avoid the capitalization rule may be available as discussed below. Livestock held for slaughter is not subject to the capitalization rule and prior law rules for costs of acquiring or creating standing timber have not been changed. The exception for plants or animals with a preproductive period of two years or less does not apply to tax shelters and corporations (or partnerships with corporate partners) which are required to use the accrual method under separate statutes.

Under the general rule, costs incurred during the preproductive period must be capitalized. According to Committee Reports, the preproductive period for an animal begins at the time of acquisition, breeding, or embryo implantation, and the period ends when the animal is ready to perform its intended function. For example, the preproductive period for a breeding cow ends when the first calf is dropped.

Under an exception to the capitalization requirement, farmers may elect to claim current deductions for the preproductive period, but the election may not be made by tax shelters, farming corporations or partnerships with corporate partners that are otherwise required to use the accrual method. The election to deduct preproductive costs currently does not apply to costs attributable to planting, cultivating, maintaining, or developing citrus or almond groves which are incurred before the end of the fourth taxable year after planting. Further, the current deduction election is not available for pistachio nut planting, maintenance, or development costs. If the election is made, the deducted costs are recaptured as ordinary income on the disposition of the product. Further, a straight-line method of depreciation (under the new alternative depreciation system) must also be elected for all farm assets placed in service in any year the election is in effect. The election to claim the current deduction must be made for the first taxable year beginning after 1986 during which a farming business is engaged in. Once made, the election applies to all future years when the IRS allows a revocation.

For purposes of the preproductive expense rules, farming includes the nursery or sod farm or the raising or harvesting of trees bearing fruits, nuts, or other crops; it does not include the raising, harvesting, or growing of timber or ornamental evergreen trees that are more than six years old at the time they are severed from the roots.

Under the new law, replanting and maintenance costs incurred following loss of or damage to an orchard, grove, or vineyard used in the production of crops for human consumption by reason of freezing temperatures, disease, droughts, pests, or casualty are deductible, even though replanting does not take place on the same property. Thus, costs incurred at a different location within the United States but by the same farmer may qualify, provided they do not relate to acreage in excess of that on which the loss or damage occurred. The provision applies to costs incurred after October 21, 1986.

Persons other than the person who owned the damaged grove, orchard, or vineyard at the time of the loss or damage may also take the deduction provided: (1) the taxpayer who owned the property at the time of loss keeps an equity interest of more than 50 percent in the property, and (2) the person claiming the deduction owns part of the remaining equity interest and materially participates in the replanting, cultivating, maintenance, or development of the property. This rule is effective for costs incurred after October 21, 1986.

The special rule for preproductive period expenses following loss or damage due to freezing temperatures or other casualty applies only in the case of crops that are normally eaten or drunk by humans. Thus, for example, jojoba bean production does not qualify under this special exception.

INTANGIBLE DRILLING COSTS

Under the prior law intangible drilling and development costs generally could be expensed or capitalized at the election of the operator of an oil, gas, or geothermal property. In the case of integrated producers, 80 percent of such costs could be expensed and the remaining 20 percent was amortized over a 36-month period beginning with the month the costs are paid or incurred. Costs of a nonproductive well (''dry hole'') were deducted currently by any taxpayer in the year the dry hole is completed.

Under the new law, 70 percent of intangible drilling costs of integrated producers may be expensed and the remaining 30 percent are to be amortized ratably over a 60-month period, beginning in the month the costs are paid or incurred. This provision does not affect the option to expense dry hole costs in the year the dry hole is completed. The provision applies to costs paid or incurred after December 31, 1986.

Intangible drilling costs incurred outside of the United States are recovered: (1) over a 10-year, straight-line amortization schedule, or (2) at the election of the operator, as part of the basis for cost depletion. This provision applies to costs paid or incurred after December 31, 1986. A transitional exception is provided for certain licenses for North Sea development acquired on or before December 31, 1985.

REVOKING AN ELECTION
TO TREAT TIMBER CUTTINGS
AS CAPITAL GAIN

Under prior law, income received on account of a retained economic interest in timber qualified for capital gains treatment, if the timber was held for more than six months before disposition. The owner of timber (or a contract right to cut timber) could elect to treat the cutting of the timber as a sale or exchange qualifying for long-term capital gains treatment, even though the timber was sold or used in the taxpayer's trade or business. Such an election was revocable only with the permission of the Secretary of the Treasury and if permission to revoke the election was granted, a new election also required the Secretary of the Treasury's consent. For purposes of these rules, timber included evergreen trees that are more than six years old at the time severed from the roots and are sold for ornamental purposes.

Since, under the new law, capital gains after 1986 will no longer be taxed at preferential rates, income from the sale of timber is generally taxable as ordinary income after 1986. However, under the new law, any prior election to treat the cutting of timber as a sale may be revoked without Treasury permission. If the election is revoked without permission and later a new election is made, any future revocations will require Treasury permission.

ADVANCE ROYALTY PAYMENTS

Under a 1984 Supreme Court decision, percentage depletion could be based on oil and gas lease bonuses or advance royalty payments. Under the new law, percentage depletion is not allowed for lease bonuses, advance royalties, or other payments made without regard to actual production from an oil, gas, or geothermal property. This is effective for amounts received or accrued after August 16, 1986.

DISPOSITION OF OIL, GAS OR GEOTHERMAL PROPERTY

Under prior law, expensed intangible drilling costs incurred after 1975 are recaptured as ordinary income upon disposition of an oil, gas, or geothermal property, to the extent of the excess of such costs over the amount that would have been deducted if the costs had been capitalized and recovered through depletion deductions.

The new law expands the recapture provision. In addition to expensed intangible drilling costs, depletion deductions which reduced the basis of oil, gas, or geothermal property are also recaptured as ordinary income when the property is disposed of. The new recapture rule applies to dispositions of property placed in service after December 31, 1986, unless acquired under a binding contract as of September 25, 1985.

REPORTING REQUIREMENTS AND TAX PRACTICE

IDENTIFICATION NUMBER OF DEPENDENT CHILD

If you claim dependency exemptions for a dependent child age five or older, you will have to obtain a Social Security number for the child and report the number on your tax returns for 1987 and later years. An exception is allowed to members of religious groups exempt from Social Security taxes.

The IRS may impose a $5 penalty for each failure to report the number or for reporting an incorrect number. However, the penalty may be avoided by showing reasonable cause for the failure.

REPORTING TAX-EXEMPT INTEREST

Starting with your 1987 return, you will have to list the amount of tax-exempt interest received. Under prior law, only taxpayers with taxable Social Security benefits were required to indicate their tax-exempt interest, although the IRS form instructions also asked for listing in Schedule B.

REAL ESTATE SALES REPORTED TO IRS

Under the new law, all real estate transactions will have to be reported to the IRS if the closing on the contract occurs on or after January 1, 1987. The attorney or other person who is responsible for closing the transaction will file the report on Form 1099-B, with a copy sent to the seller and buyer.

The Treasury is to issue guidelines specifying who is responsible for reporting the sale in cases where it is unclear who is responsible for closing the transaction.

HOUSING CO-OPS
MUST REPORT
MORTGAGE INTEREST PAYMENTS

The law requires banks and other mortgage lenders to file an information return with the IRS (and give you a copy) if your interest payments for the year are $600 or more. The report gives the IRS a check on deductions claimed for mortgage interest.

The new law requires cooperative housing corporations to report to the IRS each tenant-stockholder's share of the co-op's mortgage interest payments. The provision is retroactive to payments after 1984.

FEDERAL CONTRACTS
REPORTED TO IRS

If you have a contract with a Federal executive agency after 1986, that agency will file a report with the IRS, identifying you and including your Social Security number. All contracts signed after 1986 are subject to reporting, as are contracts signed before January 1, 1987, if still in effect on that date. The Treasury has the authority to issue regulations extending the reporting requirement to licenses granted by Federal agencies and to subcontracts that are under contracts which themselves are subject to reporting.

REPORTING ROYALTY PAYMENTS

Royalty payments in 1986 (or earlier years) had to be reported to the Treasury only if they exceeded $600.

Under the new law, royalty payments made after 1986 of $10 or more must be reported by the payer to the IRS. A person who receives royalties on behalf of another individual as a nominee must also file a report.

The reporting rules apply to royalties in intangible property such as copyrights or books as well as royalties for interests in oil, gas, coal, or other natural resources.

The information return must be given to the IRS by the end of February in the year after the year of payment. A copy of the return or similar written statement must be provided to the payee by the end of January in the year after the year of payment.

If the payee does not provide the payer with his or her Social Security number, the payer must withhold payments under backup withholding rules.

HIGHER INTEREST RATE FOR DEFICIENCIES THAN FOR TAX REFUNDS

Under prior law, the IRS paid the same interest rate on refunds as taxpayers paid on tax deficiencies. The new law allows the IRS to pay one percent less, effective for periods after 1986.

The new rate on tax deficiencies is three percentage points more than the Federal short-term rate, based on average market yields for U.S. securities maturing in three years or less. On refunds, the IRS pays only two points more than the Federal short-term rate. The rates change quarterly, with the rate for each quarter determined by the short-term rate in the first month of the previous quarter. Thus, the short-term rate in April determines the interest rate for the next quarter which includes the months of July through September.

PENALTY FOR LATE PAYMENT OF TAX

A taxpayer who files a return but does not pay the tax shown on the return is generally subject to a monthly penalty of 0.5 percent with a maximum penalty of 25 percent. The same penalty applies to taxpayers who fail to pay taxes *not* shown on the return within 10 days of notice and demand for payment by the IRS.

The new law allows the IRS to double the monthly penalty to one percent after repeated IRS requests and a notice of levy. The higher penalty can be assessed after December 31, 1986. Specifically, the increased penalty applies starting in the month after the earlier of these IRS notices: (1) A notice that the IRS will levy upon the taxpayer's assets within 10 days unless payment is made or (2) a notice demanding immediate payment where the IRS believes collection of the tax is in jeopardy. If the tax is not paid after such a demand for immediate payment, the IRS may levy upon a taxpayer's assets without waiting 10 days.

Under prior law, a taxpayer who did not file a tax return on time and who was also subject to the penalty for failing to pay taxes (not shown on a return) within 10 days of demand could reduce the failure to pay penalty by the late filing penalty. The new law repeals this offset rule.

NEGLIGENCE AND FRAUD PENALTIES

Before the new law, failure to include interest or dividend income from an information return (Form 1099) on your tax return was presumed to be negligence and subject to a five percent penalty unless you could prove you were not negligent. For returns due after 1986, including 1986 returns due in April 1987, this negligence rule is extended to amounts shown on other types of information returns, such as proceeds from a stock sale reported on Form 1099-B.

The new law retains the prior law rule that if *any* part of a tax underpayment is due to negligence, the 5 percent penalty applies to the entire underpayment and not just to the portion attributable to the negligence. Thus, if a taxpayer underpays his tax by $1,000 and the portion due to negligence is $200, the penalty is $50 (five percent of $1,000).

If a taxpayer's underpayment is due partly to negligence and partly to fraud, the negligence penalty will not apply to the portion subject to the fraud penalty. Prior law did not include such a limitation.

The fraud penalty rate is increased from 50 percent to 75 percent for returns due after 1986 (including 1986 returns) but the scope of the penalty is generally reduced to the portion of the tax underpayment due to fraud. Under prior law, the penalty applied to the entire underpayment even if only a part of it was due to fraud. Under the new law, once the IRS determines that there has been some fraud, the taxpayer can limit the penalty by showing that a portion of the underpayment is not due to fraud. The unlimited statute of limitations period will continue to apply where a return is fraudulent in any respect, even though the taxpayer may be able to limit the penalty. As under prior law, if fraud is shown on a joint return, the penalty only applies to the tax of a spouse who has committed the fraud.

Further, the new law retains the rule that increases the negligence and fraud penalties by 50 percent of the interest payable on the portion of the underpayment due to the negligence or fraud.

SUBSTANTIAL UNDERPAYMENT OF TAX

You are subject to a penalty where you understate tax liability on a return by the greater of $5,000 or 10 percent of the proper tax. The 1986 Tax Act, signed into law on October 22, 1986, increased the penalty from 10 percent to 20 percent, effective for returns due after 1986 without regard to extensions. However, the day before, on October 21, a budget bill was signed into law which repealed the Tax Act provision and increased the penalty to 25 percent, effective for penalties assessed after October 21, 1986. Since the Tax Act became law a day later, the 20 percent penalty rate technically applies. However, the Treasury plans to apply the 25 percent penalty and will press Congress for a technical correction repealing the 20 percent rate. The 25 percent penalty can be retroactively applied to returns for prior years where the statute of limitations is still open.

As under prior law, the penalty can generally be avoided by providing on your return a statement of facts disclosing your position, or by showing that your position was substantially supported by tax authority such as statutes, regulations, court decisions, or rulings. However, for understatements of liability due to tax shelter items, the penalty may be avoided only if there is substantial authority for your position and you reasonably believed that your position was more likely than not correct.

PENALTY FOR FAILURE
TO FILE INFORMATION RETURNS

Higher penalties apply if information returns due after 1986 (without extensions) are not timely or adequately filed.

Failure to provide a required information return to the IRS or a required statement to a payee, such as wage or interest statements, will be subject to a $50 penalty for each failure, with a maximum annual penalty of $100,000. Under an exception, the IRS will not impose penalties for failures due to reasonable cause and not willful neglect.

The $50 penalty may be increased to $100 for failures due to intentional disregard of filing requirements, and for specific reporting requirements, the penalty could be still higher. For example, if business cash payments exceeding $10,000 are intentionally not reported, the penalty would be 10 percent of the reportable amount if that exceeded the $100 penalty. Further, for such intentional failures to file, there is no ceiling on the penalty.

For filing an incorrect or incomplete information return to the IRS or payee, a penalty of up to $5 per return with a limit of $20,000 per year could be imposed unless reasonable cause is shown. As with intentional failures to file a required return, higher penalties with no annual penalty ceiling apply where returns are intentionally made incomplete.

Penalties on payers of interest and dividends are not subject to the $20,000 or $100,000 annual ceiling; and to avoid penalties, such payers must show due diligence and not just reasonable cause.

LEGAL FEE AWARDS

The rules for recovery of attorney's fees and other litigation costs have been changed for cases begun after 1985. Generally, prevailing taxpayers who have exhausted all administrative remedies within the IRS may recover up to $75 an hour for attorneys' fees by proving that the IRS position was not substantially justified. An award may be based on unjustified conduct by the IRS District Council during pre-trial administrative proceedings as well as on IRS conduct after litigation begins.

The $75 per hour recovery for attorneys' fees replaced the $25,000 cap under prior law. The $75 rate may be increased if the court determines that a higher rate is justified.

You may also recover reasonable fees, based on prevailing market rates for expert witnesses and special reports, such as an engineer's report necessary to the preparation of your case. However, the recovery for expert witnesses may not exceed the amount paid by the Government to its own expert witnesses.

TAX COURT PRACTICE FEE

Under prior law, a practitioner was required to pay a $25 application fee before being admitted to practice before the IRS. No periodic re-registration fee was required.

The new law authorizes the Tax Court to impose a registration fee of not more than $30 annually starting January 1, 1987.

The fees are to be used by the court to conduct disciplinary proceedings against practitioners who violate court rules.

TAX COURT PENALTY
EXTENDED

Under prior law, the Tax Court could impose a penalty of up to $5,000 if it concluded that your position was frivolous or that you brought the action primarily to delay payment of your taxes.

For cases begun after October 22, 1986, the penalty may also be imposed if you unreasonably failed to pursue available administrative remedies with the IRS.

PROJECTING THE TAX CONSEQUENCES OF THE NEW LAW

You now know details of the new law. With the following work-sheets, you can determine how you will fare—whether you will pay less or more, or the same amount of taxes. Important changes in the law are highlighted next to affected tax items.

TAX COMPARISON WORK SHEETS

Income	1986	1987	1988
(Include spouse's income if filing jointly)			
Compensation	$_____	$_____	$_____
Interest	_____	_____	_____
Dividends (no $100/$200 exclusion after 1986)	_____	_____	_____
Capital gain (less 60% of long-term capital gain in 1986, fully taxable afterwards)	_____	_____	_____
Unemployment compensation (fully taxable after 1986)	_____	_____	_____
Rent and Royalties (passive losses are not applied against other income after 1986)	_____	_____	_____
Partnership loss (passive losses are not applied against other income after 1986)	_____	_____	_____
Scholarship and grants (may be taxable after 1986)	_____	_____	_____
All other income	_____	_____	_____
Total Step 1	$_____	$_____	$_____

Adjustments	1986	1987	1988
Employee expenses (unreimbursed travel costs deductible after 1986 as itemized deduction subject to 2% AGI floor,	$_____	$_____	$_____
IRA deduction (may not be deductible in 1987 depending on income and company coverage)	_____	_____	_____
Married couple earner deduction (not after 1986)	_____	_____	_____
Other adjustments (moving expenses deductible here in 1986; itemized after 1986)	_____	_____	_____
Total Step 2	$_____	$_____	$_____

Itemized deductions	1986	1987	1988
Medical and dental (5% AGI floor in 1986; 7.5% after 1986)	$_____	$_____	$_____
Contributions	_____	_____	_____
State and local income tax	_____	_____	_____
Property tax	_____	_____	_____
Sales tax (not deductible after 1986)	_____	_____	_____
Consumer interest (65% deductible in 1987, 40% in 1988)	_____	_____	_____
Investment interest (65% deductible in 1987)	_____	_____	_____
Mortgage interest (restrictions after 1986)	_____	_____	_____
Casualty and theft losses (exceeding 10% AGI)	_____	_____	_____
Miscellaneous nonbusiness expenses (less 2% AGI floor after 1986)	_____	_____	_____
Minus zero bracket amount in 1986	_____		

Other deductions

Nonitemized charitable donation deduction (not deductible after 1986)	——		
Standard deduction (if you do not itemize after 1986		——	——
Total Step 3	$___	$___	$___

Summary	1986	1987	1988
Income Step 1	$___	$___	$___
Less Step 2 Adjustments	(___)	(___)	(___)
Step 3 Itemized Deductions	(___)	(___)	(___)
Less Exemptions __ × $1,080 (1986;age/blind extra)	(___)		
__ × $1,900 (1987)		(___)	
__ × $1,950 (1988)			(___)
Taxable Income	$___	$___	$___

EXAMPLE—

You and your spouse work and file a joint return. Your salary in 1986 is $50,000; your spouse earns $32,000. You have interest income of $2,000, dividend income of $1,200 and net long-term capital gains of $10,000. You and your spouse contribute $2,000 each to an IRA. You are both covered by company retirement plans. You make charitable donations of $1,000, pay $2,000 in real estate taxes, $3,000 interest on your home mortgage, $300 interest on consumer loans, and $700 in state and local sales taxes. You also had $300 of investment and unreimbursed job-related expenses. You also have a tax shelter loss of $5,000.

Here is a comparison of your tax liability in 1986, 1987, and 1988 taking into account the new law changes and assuming the same income and expenses for each of the three years. Under the new law, no IRA, married couple earner, sales tax, and capital gain deductions are allowed, the consumer interest deduction is reduced, and miscellaneous deductions are not deductible because of the 2% AGI floor.

Income	1986	1987	1988
Salary	$ 82,000	$ 82,000	$ 82,000
Dividends	1,000	1,200	1,200
Interest	2,000	2,000	2,000
Capital gain	4,000	10,000	10,000
Loss	(5,000)		
Step 1 Income	$ 84,000	$ 95,200	$ 95,200
Less IRA deduction	(4,000)		
Married couple earner deduction	(3,000)		
Step 2 Adjustments	(7,000)		

Itemized deductions	1986	1987	1988
Charitable donation	$ 1,000	$ 1,000	$ 1,000
Real estate taxes	2,000	2,000	2,000
Mortgage interest	3,000	3,000	3,000
Consumer interest	300	195	120
Sales tax	700		
Miscellaneous job and investment expense	300	*	*
	$ 7,300		
Less 1986 ZBA	3,670		
Step 3 Deductions	$ 3,630	$ 6,195	$ 6,120

Summary	1986	1987	1988
Step 1	$ 84,000	$ 95,200	$ 95,200
Less Step 2	(7,000)		
Step 3	(3,630)	(6,195)	(6,120)
Step 4	(2,160)	(3,800)	(3,900)
Taxable Income	$ 71,210	$ 85,205	$ 85,180
Tax	$ 19,082	22,912**	20,646

*Does not exceed 2% ceiling of adjusted gross income.
**Tax will be about $700 less than $22,912 after taking into account the 1987 capital gain adjustment for 28% rate.

1986 TAX RATES

SINGLE (1986)

If taxable income is— Not over $2,440		Tax is— —0—	Plus following percentage	of the amount over
Over—	but not over—			
$ 2,480	$ 3,670		11%	$ 2,480
3,670	4,750	$ 130.90	12	3,670
4,750	7,010	260.50	14	4,750
7,010	9,170	576.90	15	7,010
9,170	11,650	900.90	16	9,170
11,650	13,920	1,297.70	18	11,650
13,920	16,190	1,706.30	20	13,920
16,190	19,640	2,160.30	23	16,190
19,640	25,360	2,953.80	26	19,640
25,360	31,080	4,441.00	30	25,360
31,080	36,800	6,157.00	34	31,080
36,800	44,780	8,101.80	38	36,800
44,780	59,670	11,134.20	42	44,780
59,670	88,270	17,388.00	48	59,670
88,270		31,116.00	50	88,270

JOINT RETURN (1986)

If taxable income is— Not over $3,670		Tax is— —0—	Plus following percentage	of the amount over
Over—	but not over—			
$ 3,670	$ 5,940		11%	$ 3,670
5,940	8,200	$ 249.70	12	5,940
8,200	12,840	520.90	14	8,200
12,840	17,270	1,170.50	16	12,840
17,270	21,800	1,879.30	18	17,270
21,800	26,550	2,694.70	22	21,800
26,550	32,270	3,739.70	25	26,550
32,270	37,980	5,169.70	28	32,270
37,980	49,420	6,768.50	33	37,980
49,420	64,750	10,543.70	38	49,420
64,750	92,370	16,369.10	42	64,750
92,370	118,050	27,969.50	45	92,370
118,050	175,250	39,525.50	49	118,050
175,250		67,553.50	50	175,250

1986 TAX RATES (cont.)

HEAD OF HOUSEHOLD (1986)

If taxable income is— Not over $2,480 Over—	but not over—		Tax is— —0— Plus following percentage	of the amount over
$ 2,480	$ 4,750		11%	$ 2,480
4,750	7,010	$ 249.70	12	4,750
7,010	9,390	520.90	14	7,010
9,390	12,730	854.10	17	9,390
12,730	16,190	1,421.90	18	12,730
16,190	19,640	2,044.70	20	16,190
19,640	25,360	2,734.70	24	19,640
25,360	31,080	4,107.50	28	25,360
31,080	36,800	5,709.10	32	31,080
36,800	48,240	7,539.50	35	36,800
48,240	65,390	11,543.50	42	48,240
65,390	88,270	18,746.50	45	65,390
88,270	116,870	29,042.50	48	88,270
116,870		42,770.50	50	116,870

1987 TAX RATES

JOINT RETURN (1987)

If taxable income is—		Tax is	Plus following percent	of amount over
Over—	but not over—			
$ 0	$ 3,000		11%	$ 0
3,000	28,000	$ 330	15	3,000
28,000	45,000	4,080	28	28,000
45,000	90,000	8,840	35	45,000
90,000		24,590	38.5	90,000

SINGLE (1987)

If taxable income is—		Tax is	Plus following percent	of amount over
Over—	but not over—			
$ 0	$ 1,800		11%	$ 0
1,800	16,800	$ 198	15	1,800
16,800	27,000	2,448	28	16,800
27,000	54,000	5,304	35	27,000
54,000		14,754	38.5	54,000

HEAD OF HOUSEHOLD (1987)

If taxable income is—		Tax is	Plus following percent	of amount over
Over—	but not over—			
$ 0	$ 2,500		11%	$ 0
2,500	23,000	$ 275	15	2,500
23,000	38,000	3,350	28	23,000
38,000	80,000	7,550	35	38,000
80,000		22,250	38.5	80,000

1988 TAX RATES

JOINT RETURN (1988)

If taxable income is—		Tax is	Plus following percent	of amount over
Over—	but not over—			
$ 0	$ 29,750		15%	$ 0
29,750	71,900	$ 4,462.50	28	29,750
71,900	149,250	16,264.50	33*	71,900
149,250			28**	0

SINGLE (1988)

If taxable income is—		Tax is	Plus following percent	of amount over
Over—	but not over—			
$ 0	$17,850		15%	$ 0
17,850	43,150	$ 2,677.50	28	17,850
43,150	89,560	9,761.50	33*	43,150
89,560			28**	0

HEAD OF HOUSEHOLD (1988)

If taxable income is—		Tax is	Plus following percent	of amount over
Over—	but not over—			
$ 0	$ 23,900		15%	$ 0
23,900	61,650	$ 3,585	28	23,900
61,650	123,790	14,155	33*	61,650
123,790			28**	0

*Reflects 5% surtax phasing out 15% rate benefit on part of your taxable income.
**Flat tax of 28% on all taxable income. Further, add 5% surtax phasing out tax benefit of personal and dependent exemptions. The surtax is the lower of (a) $546 times number of exemptions or (b) 5% of (taxable income - $149,250) on joint return; 5% of (taxable income - $89,560) on single return; 5% of (taxable income - $123,790) on head of household return.